Reflections of Guernsey

by

Molly Bihet

With Best Wishes
Molly Bihet.

REFLECTIONS OF GUERNSEY

ISBN 0 9510619 1 7

PRINTING HISTORY
First published October 1993

Copies of 'A Child's War',
and 'Reflections of Guernsey'
1940 to 1993 available by post from
Molly Bihet
Woodcote, 35 Les Canichers,
St Peter Port, Guernsey, Channel Islands, GY1 2LS
Tel. 0481 722996

Price each copy £3.50 including post & packing.

Printed by The Guernsey Press Co. Ltd.,
Guernsey, Channel Islands.

Front cover pictures
'A Child's War'
Mother selling poppies

CONTENTS

Was *'Bullneck'* the dreaded Nazi *'Otto'*?

From Page 14*

'Werner Hostmann' of the German Occupying Forces re-lives his stay on Guernsey and Sark from 1943 to 1946.

From Page 106*

Through my writing 'A Child's War' and my meeting with another German, a remarkable story of bravery has come to light. 'Erich Wegner' saved 84 British Sailors after the sinking of 'H.M.S. Gloucester' off Crete in 1941. (one such survivor being a Guernseyman).

From Pages 102-106*

PREFACE

I have been asked so many times for a follow up to 'A Child's War' and not really having an excuse for not doing so — here it is. The success of my last book of course was the simplicity of it and the great character of my mother who made the reading of it lighthearted, even though we lost our freedom on the Island of Guernsey from June 1940 to May 1945. The Channel Islands were the only British Territory to be occupied by thousands of German Troops during this time. Instances have come to light and statistics of those Occupation Days will be of interest I am sure, also the rehabilitation period and the home coming of thousands and coincidences which have occurred since 1985 with the printing of 'A Child's War'. Towards the end of the book and the end of my dear mother's life, another coincidence which in a way, made for her contented passing.

ACKNOWLEDGEMENTS

My appreciation and sincere thanks to a much loved and respected Guernseyman 'Sir John Loveridge' former Bailiff of Guernsey (1973 to 1982) for the Foreword he wrote to 'A Child's War'.

For 'Reflections' my sincere thanks to Mr Brian Clegg and staff at the Guernsey Press Company also for permission to reproduce copyright material. To Sue Fryer of Brize Norton, Oxon. To Mr Ken Tough of the Channel Islands Occupation Society and Mr W. Gallienne of the Islands Archives Services.

To Mr W. (Bill) Bougourd, Mr Alf Le Poidevin, Mr E. (Ted) Hill and Mr Paul Le Pelley. To Joan Stockdale of Sark and to Irene Ruthven, not forgetting her son John who over the years had designed, made and sent me appropriate birthday cards, now printed!

1940 1945

"Now we have our
foot inside the
door of the
British Empire"

ADOLF HITLER

Führer HQ

June 30th 1940

ALDERNEY

GUERNSEY HERM
LIHOU JETHOU
BRÉCHOU SARK

JERSEY

"Cease fire began
yesterday . . . .
and our dear
Channel Islands
are to be liberated"

WINSTON CHURCHILL
House of Commons
May 8th 1945

Royal Message to the Channel Islands

BUCKINGHAM PALACE
June 24th, 1940

To the Bailiffs of Jersey and Guernsey.

For strategic reasons, it has been found necessary to withdraw the Armed Forces from the Channel Islands.

I deeply regret this necessity, and I wish to assure My people in the Islands that in taking this decision, My Government have not been unmindful of their position. It is in their interest that this step should be taken in present circumstances.

The long association of the Islands with the Crown and the loyal service the people of the Islands have rendered to My Ancestors and Myself are guarantees that the link between us will remain unbroken, and I know the My people in the Islands will look forward with the same confidence as I do to the day when the resolute fortitude with which we face our precent difficulties will reap the reward of Victory.

GEORGE R. I.

CHAPTER 1

HOW IT ALL BEGAN!

I was born in 1931 — my sister in 1933 to William Joseph (Bill) Finigan and Gladys Elsie (née Collins), all born in St. Peter Port, Guernsey and also André Pierre Joseph Bihet whom I married in 1954. We have enjoyed a happy and contented life together like my mother and father had before us.

We have two daughters, Sally is married to Michael Howlett, Carole to Geoffrey Cottam. (Both families living in Guernsey). We have four grand-children, Carly and Ryan, Naomi and Joshua.

Now for them and for the many readers who have wanted a follow up to 'A Child's War' at long last here it is. . . . .

I have had great satisfaction in writing, and my story 'A Child's War' has been read by many thousands of people. I have lost count of the letters I have received thanking me for writing down in simple terms what family life was really like during those dark days of German occupation. It has been rewarding hearing from so many people who I look upon as friends and also so many old acquaintances and old school friends who have taken the time to write. Many had left Guernsey shores and had written from the mainland and from all over the world. All just wanted to write and usually finished their letters with "Do hope your mother is well".

Even through my small book, her character shone through and so many admired how she coped and looked after the family of nine with such shortages. Because of the respect and love I had for my mother and father, I have never forgotten the anxious and worrying times they had to face from 1940 to 1945 and can always remember my mother telling our mainland guests who stayed with us, that one day she would write down her experiences of that period and write her story. As time went by, she lost the enthusiasm I expect and it was about ten to twelve years ago that I started putting pen to paper and also told my guests that one day, 'I'll see my book in print,' and they all agreed it should be done. It was not until early in 1985 when the fortieth anniversary of our Liberation was looming and the celebrations and thoughts were in everyone's minds that I decided it was now or never.

Through my good friend of many years, Irene Ruthven encouraging me and when seeing in the Guernsey Evening Press — 'Experiences of the German Occupation' required for the purpose of compiling records for a new book, this sparked off my interest again and from then on, I really got down to work. It was fairly easy for me to write as during the five years of occupation, the memory of it all was very clear and has always remained fresh. When one gets older, the memory does start to fade and seeing the slight change gradually coming to my mother's memory, I wanted to get my feelings down before I also got too old. There were to be several similar books coming out around Liberation (1985) so I was advised perhaps to have the printing done at my own expense.

Time was running short anyway as I had left the writing to the last minute so to speak. There was no point having books for sale after May 9th (not in my mind) and I was determined to get it done. André (my better half) encouraged me too; also after the director of the Paramount Lithoprint (who printed the First Edition) had looked and read it, he was also convinced readers would find 'A Child's War' interesting. The title was a thought from Irene's son, John Ruthven, who also gave me an idea for the beach scene on the front cover. Thanks John, although it did cause a few headaches! I had a vision of what I wanted to see on the front, so duly borrowed and was kindly lent the German jackboot from Mr. Richard Heaume of the German Occupation Museum (well worth a visit), I made a swastika from paper, was given a beach 'pre-war' rubber bucket from Irene's mum and with the Union Jack and an old teddy bear, André and I were set to go. The first time we ventured to a beach was with a good friend Ted Hill who had acquired a new, expensive and reliable camera (or so we thought!). At Vazon it would not work at all!

The next time André and I went down to Grandes Rocques Bay, André wearing the boots (after lots of difficulty getting them on) and then unfortunately the photographs just did not turn out at all! We were beginning to think we were jinxed as although the photographs did turn out the next time, they just did not look right.

The very next fine and clear day, I decided to go it alone and took the car to Grandes Havres looking out towards Chouet with the German tower in the background. The picture I thought would be promising. Strangely though this tower has recently fallen and collapsed into the quarry beneath and the only one on the Island which has given way which I like to think makes my picture rather special and unique. Whilst making the sandcastle and placing the swastika on the top, an elderly gentleman passed by and looking rather disgusted said to me 'swastikas are not liked on the Island so why was I playing with it?' I had to smile and told him it was for a cover of a book I was writing. He walked on but I doubt very much he believed me, and said nothing.

The last visit to the beach proved to be good and the front cover was chosen — now was the time to decide how many copies to be printed. I was advised to print at least a 1,000! Oh dear! I only really wanted 500 but understood it was a costly business and only 500 would cost far more than the retail price. All through this new venture, Valerie Falla who worked at the Paramount Lithoprint was very helpful and I appreciated her help and patience, even when my writing sometimes was scribbly and more thoughts had come to mind. Thinking back, I was rather ignorant in these new business matters and wondered whether 1,000 books would sell. Hopefully, I thought they would go eventually. As it happened, within six weeks, the whole 1,000 copies had been distributed and sold and another order was given quickly.

Since that time, I have had several reprints at the Guernsey Press Company but there was a funny episode when I had ordered a further reprint of 7,000 copies! I was out when a young carpenter who was working at home and who answered the telephone, was asked by the Guernsey Press Company whether he was able to accept a parcel of books, little did he know of the quantity that was coming! The van was still parked outside the house when I returned and the poor carpenter was almost on his knees! He was in a bit of a panic too, as he did not know where to stack them all — relief when he saw me and then a good laugh together. Imagine his surprised look expecting a small parcel and then seeing all those books to be moved from the van!

Apart from the cover of the book and the photograph, many other questions are put to me at the Olde Guernsey Market where I have come into contact with many who have read 'A Child's War'. I have tried to answer some — why did I sign Sarnia Cherie at the back? (Translated it means 'Guernsey Dear'). It is really Guernsey's National Anthem so to speak. Whenever Guernsey people are gathered together, this song seems to bring everyone closer, especially when away from home and perhaps with sadness, longing for home. It was sung by the many people who were evacuated to the mainland during the war at their regular Channel Island meetings and even now, in all parts of the world when local folk are gathered together, tears come easily when singing this song, which I am sure happened to everyone exiled away and parted from their loved ones in the past.

Chorus words —

Sarnia Cherie, Gem of the Sea,
Home of my childhood,
My heart yearns for thee,
Thy voice calls me ever,
Forget thee I'll never,
Island of Beauty, Sarnia Cherie.

Noted Guernsey Composer
of Sarnia Cherie
Signor Dominique Santangelo

Guernsey is a past Norman French name and means 'Green Island'.

CHAPTER 2

OCCUPATION & QUESTIONS ANSWERED
— Do You? Did They?

Another question 'Do any of the Germans ever come back?' and the answer is yes but I am sure they must be the good Germans! From time to time there have been photographs in our local newspaper of a German ex-soldier who has returned and met up with a local person he had befriended and helped during the Occupation. Many I am sure thought this Island and their stay was heaven (see later on), especially before 1944. There were a few who came back to live in the Island after the war. They had met and eventually married Guernsey girls and now have families.

Also of course, we had thousands of prisoners of war working here. One we have known well for many years fell in love and married a local girl during this time, having had special permission to do so. He was Spanish and together with his father was forced to come to Guernsey in 1942. They worked side by side on the very large Mirus Battery at the Frie Baton, St. Saviour's. These poor men led a very miserable existence and there was no way they could be openly helped by the Islanders — again it was 'verboten'.

Different garrisons of German troops came and went at the beginning of the occupation and at any one time. There were many thousands of German Forces on the Island, also Prisoners of War who were working (usually day and night) and dying on building the fortifications, tunnels, gun emplacements etc. all over the Island. Guernsey was far more fortified than the other Channel Islands.

Some 60,000 mines were laid on the cliffs and around our shores. Only last year an S-mine was again found on the cliffs and this year (1993) a large 500 lb bomb (5' x 2' diameter) was found on the sea bed 500 yards from the St. Peter Port Harbour Signal Station. The bomb was exploded by the Royal Navy underwater clearance team.

With the building of these fortifications and strongpoints, transporting materials of all kinds — steel, timber, cement, ammunition, equipment, fuel and food etc, within the Islands were most important, almost equal to the shipping that brought all the imported materials that arrived from the Continent. Also within the Islands many thousands of tons of sand and granite from the beaches were moved about the Island for building fortifications and railways.

Yes, we had a railway — built to carry all these materials starting at the harbour at St. Peter Port to the north at St. Sampson's, then to L'Ancresse and around the west coast to L'Eree and to just beyond Rocquaine Bay to strong points and gun sites nearby. The railway apparently was stopped after knocking down the gable of a house on the Perelle Coast road. The railways were built over fields, through vineyards and gardens and if houses were in the Germans' path, they were knocked down too. Also, as in Jersey, the railway was built to go around approximately two thirds of the coast line but not to the hilly cliffs on our own south coast.

There was never any public mention of what was going on in the Island, so living in the town and with no transport, we did not realise quite what was going on, we only used to watch the trucks and wagons and hopefully wait for perhaps a bag of cement to fall off into the road along the Esplanade for my sister and I to collect! (A Child's War).

So many also ask how we Islanders feel towards the German tourists who visit Guernsey now. At the time when the Germans landed and took over Guernsey they were all hated and feared too. With living in a small community everyone remembered the 'raid' on the Harbour and knew personally someone who had been killed or injured by machine guns. Gradually life settled down and islanders knew they had to accept they were the 'Top Dogs' and to accept the orders that were given out almost daily. Gradually the Islanders learnt to live the different almost boring routine, but in a very close way with each other. Generally I believe now the majority of the 60 year old 'plus' who are getting fewer and fewer on the Island bear no malice. After the Liberation everyone wanted to forget everything that had happened, now I suppose most have mellowed with age, and have accepted like every nation there were good and bad. On the whole, I do not think people resent or single them out because they are German. I was aged from nine to fourteen years during the Occupation so my idea of Germans would be different from the adult population. My husband André and I have always respected everyone we have met and have made good friends with German couples whilst on holiday abroad. When they have stayed at our guesthouse, there has been no difference in our attitude towards them. We have all shared many laughs and had them return again.

One particular couple, Heika and Winfred (Gypsy) Kraut (yes Kraut!) have been insistent we visit them in their German home. We met this couple whilst on holiday in Cyprus perhaps eight or nine years ago — made friends and they have visited Guernsey and stayed at our own home. With the delay in printing this book, we now have just returned from their home in Stuttgart and enjoyed their hospitality and genuine friendship very much (October 1992). But even at this time and after all these years I feel two or three together talking are acceptable but when surrounded by a crowd, I seem to go back in time and I do not feel at all comfortable.

At my stall at the Olde Market on Thursdays, a number of Germans on holiday have bought my book, several have got in touch and have been pleased to think I have remembered a little kindness shown by the enemy at the time. They do not like the reminder of the fortifications around the Island and do not like to see 'swastikas' as a reminder on books etc. *Only once* has a younger man been rather nasty at my stall — he left saying 'I hope you do not sell many of your books'. My answer to him and others, 'it is part of Guernsey's and the Islands history and must be told for future generations'. The stories are true and cannot be forgotten — we are fortunate now and have so much, we must never take our own good life and freedom for granted.

INTERNMENT AND DEPORTATION
1942 & 1943

Another question which comes up most weeks. Did any sabotage or resistance against the Germans take place? Again it was most difficult to try anything although there were acts that one did get away with from time to time — hence the reason why the prison was for ever full with waiting lists! In a recent published book 'Guernsey Green' I noted with interest that Bill Green did get away with it at times and he and friends tried to form a 'resistance' group. But with second thoughts it was almost impossible to do anything as really there was nowhere to hide, and if caught serious reprisals would be taken on themselves and all the family even on the Islanders. The small group that had met had to squash the idea. I remember very well, the letter 'V' seemed to appear on many houses where Germans were living. Mostly they were painted on, others were placed on walls and pillars in tar or bitumen.

Our own Special Constables were sent out with buckets and sponges to clean and clear up. 'V's (for Victory) were also cut out of paper and cardboard and left in places to annoy the Germans. Some left and placed on car seats for the Germans to find on returning, they were dropped in streets, left on shop counters, slipped into folded newspapers and pushed through letter boxes of houses occupied by Germans.

Acts like this annoyed the enemy and a reward of £25 was offered for the conviction of anyone committing these offences.

Unfortunately one Guernseyman was sentenced to five months imprisonment for being caught and he finished his term of sentence in 'Laufen' Internment Camp. Another man (besides other deeds done in the Cobo and Grandes Rocques districts) was sentenced to one year's imprisonment for chalking 'V's on the cycle seats of the German's motorbikes whilst the soldier was drinking in hotel bars. The 'V' signs could be clearly seen on the seats of their trousers and were not easy to rub off until the trousers had been taken off! Much teasing and laughter from their colleagues, but most were very angry! Apparently 19 children from the Parish School were also accused of having written 'V' signs in their districts and together with their parents and teachers were questioned before a German tribunal. They were dismissed with warnings, some 'fatherly' advice was given and threats of more serious consequences should it happen again.

Some others were not so fortunate but saying that Ron Hurford is the first to admit he was a 'wicked devil' when younger. He was aged 17-18 at the time when he got into trouble having a go at a German. He was working at a local bakehouse at the time and certainly went a bit too far, (we knew him well later as our friendly milkman!) He took the blame for his working mates who had stolen bread from the Germans and in the heat of the moment he hit out and suffered physically, and still shows the signs from the German blows to one of his eyes. He was also suffering mentally at the time. First he was placed in the Guernsey jail and had to wait 4½ months for a trial. He was then sentenced to six weeks solitary confinement which to a young man must have been pretty daunting. Later he was sent to Laufen Internment Camp. It was only recently I heard of the traumatic time he suffered and although finding it difficult to speak of his experiences and at what cruelty he'd seen at times at Laufen, he felt like others who defied the enemy the story should be recorded for posterity in the archive records of the C.I. Occupation Society.

Whilst he was in solitary Ron had no comfort whatsoever, no bed, only wood slats on the floor. He was allowed just one blanket as a covering for one night out of four nothing else (like he said it was a good thing he took in his 'Guernsey' with him.) For three days his ration of 2oz dry bread and coffee only was given, on the fourth day he was allowed a normal day's ration consisting mainly of watery soup and his blanket! In some ways although very frightened I'm sure, I suppose he was relieved to see daylight and travel on the old cattle boat to St. Malo then on to Laufen Camp. There he still maintained his high adventurous spirit and was always in trouble for a further three years until the camp was liberated by the Americans. Stories like this emerge from time to time and many islanders defied the Germans here, what a pity the 'media' do not publicise these stories and acts of courage instead of making Guernsey seem like an island of collaborators.

It is sad that since the release of files and documents (1,800) after some 47 years much sorrow has been felt by the families of the Bailiff at the time Victor Carey (later to be Sir Victor Carey) and to Jurat John Leale who was the acting President of Guernsey's Controlling Committee (the Civil Administration). As a young girl I well remember my mother and father having a great respect for both these gentlemen and for all the Governing Committee who did all they could for the good of the Islanders. Some articles written in the national newspapers have accused these two gentlemen of giving the Germans information of Jewish ladies living at the time on the Island, and sadly one 'Theresia Steiner' was known to have been gassed at 'Auschwitz'. Others also were never known to have returned from the Camp. Everyone living on the Island over the age of fourteen had to always carry an Identity Card which the Germans had insisted on everyone having complete with personal particulars and details. Having 'copies' the German Authorities were fully aware of the Jewish ladies on the Island; also should anyone in authority not have obeyed orders from the 'Commandant' reprisals would have been carried out on the residents with the threat of Islanders being shot. There has been mention of this (20 in fact) – so many things are coming to light. It must have been a most difficult time for our leaders dealing with the Enemy. There surely must have been an extremely worrying time during 1942-1943 when deportation took place of grown-ups and children to a number of camps in southern Germany for the duration of the War. This being a direct order from Adolf Hitler. When residents were first told of the forthcoming deportation at least five people committed suicide; no-one knew the outcome and what would happen being sent away to the continent. Files have also revealed that German civilians were living amongst us during and throughout the Occupation, but many had unknown jobs and were assumed to be 'secret police'.

You may be interested to read statistics and numbers kindly given by Mr. Ken Tough of the Channel Islands Occupation Society.

FACTS AND FIGURES ON THE OCCUPATION (with special reference to Guernsey, the most densely populated and most heavily fortified Channel Island)

THE CIVILIAN POPULATION – 43,820 in 1939 in 24 square miles; 19,000 left for England including most men of military age and 4,700 Island schoolchildren. 23,981 civilians remained when the Germans arrived, including 1039 schoolchildren. War deaths were:– 231 Islanders in the British armed forces in all theatres of war, 30 in the German air raid on 28th June, 1940 and 15 in Allied air raids, mine-field accidents etc. 887 were interned in Germany.

THE GERMAN GARRISON – Maximum of 13,000 in May, 1943, of whom 1850 were airmen and 1420 sailors – the latter being mostly flak and coastal artillery gunners respectively. There were more Germans per square mile in Guernsey than in Germany. 11,755 remained to be taken prisoner in 1945. 261 died during the occupation, of whom 111 are buried in the British military cemetery at Fort George, Guernsey.

THE FORCED WORKERS – Maximum of 5,100 in May, 1943, many from eastern Europe and north Africa. At least 97 are known to have died; 42 Frenchmen, 15 Algerians, 10 Belgians, 10 Dutchmen, 6 Spaniards, 2 Poles, 1 Italian, 1 Chinaman, 1 Russian, 1 Portuguese and 8 unknown. (This list is almost certainly incomplete and much research remains to be done).

THE FORTIFICATIONS – By September 1944 272,000 cubic metres of reinforced concrete had been employed in Guernsey, the majority in the spring and summer of 1942 and 1943; 76,746 mines had been sown along the coastline; 36 8.8cm flak guns and 65 other heavier artillery pieces of up to 30.5cm calibre had been emplaced.

THE PRIVATIONS OF THE CIVILIAN POPULATION – The island imported an average of 16,636 tons of food annually prior to 1940; in the last 9 months of the Occupation, when the Islands were besieged by the Allies none could be imported. The adult weekly bread ration fell from 3lbs in November, 1944 and no bread at all was available for three weeks from 13th February, 1945. Petrol consumption fell from 108,000 gallons in May, 1940 to 1872 gallons in April, 1945. The population survived thanks to fortnightly issues of prisoner-of-war food parcels supplied by the International Red Cross.

REGISTRATION FORM.

A6c-53

Two copies of this Form must be completed by every person.
If you are in doubt as to how to complete this Form, the Constable or a Douzenier of your Parish will help you.

For Official use only.

No. 3065

A1

COLLINS

(a) Surname in block letters followed by Christian names. — (a) FINIGAN *Gladys Elsie*

(j) Any physical peculiarities, such as a scar, limp, etc. — (j) Scar Throat Operation

(b) Ordinary Postal address, including Parish — (b) 30 Canichers St Peter Port

(k) Have you served in any of His Britannic Majesty's Armed Forces? If so, write R.N., R.N.R., Army, R.A.F., Royal Guernsey Militia, or as is appropriate and give your rank on retirement and the date of retirement — (k) No

(c) Date of Birth — (c) 19/10/1905

(d) Place of Birth *Guernsey* — (d) 30 Canichers

(e) Nationality* — (e) British

(l) Are you on a Reserve of Officers of His Britannic Majesty's Armed Forces? If so, state which Reserve — (l) No

(f) Occupation — (f) Housewife

(g) Single, married, widow or widower — (g) Married

(m) Are you, not being on a Reserve of Officers, on the Reserve of any of His Britannic Majesty's Armed Forces? If so, state which Reserve — (m)

(h) Colour of hair — (h) Brown

(i) Colour of eyes — (i) Blue

*As regards question (e), if you are a person possessing dual nationality, give both nationalities.

RELATIONSHIP	NAME	
Nephew	Reg Galliene	
Nephew	Lionel	Collis

(n) Have you a husband, son, grandson, brother, father, nephew, uncle, or first cousin actually serving in any of His Britannic Majesty's Armed Forces? If so, give his relationship to you and his full name and rank and state which branch (such as R.N., Army, R.A.F., or as the case may require) of the Forces he belongs to.
Do not give his Unit or any particulars of his last known whereabouts.

If this space for your answer is insufficient, complete your answer on the reverse of this Form.

RELATIONSHIP	NAME	ADDRESS
No	No	No

(o) Have you a husband, son, grandson, brother, father, nephew, uncle or first cousin who is, to your knowledge, on a Reserve of Officers of His Britannic Majesty's Armed Forces? If so, give his relationship to you and his full name and address.

(p) Having completed the answers to the above questions (and where the answer to any of them is in the negative, the word "No" must be written) take this Form to a Constable or Douzenier of your Parish (in the case of Sark, you must take it to the Seneschal) and write your usual signature in his presence and add the date.

(Signature) *Gladys E. Finigan*

(Date) 28/10/40

Your signature must be witnessed by the Official before whom it is signed and he will sign his name and add his official title and the name of the Parish of which he is an Official.

Witnessed by *John C Rouvier* (Signature)

DOUZENIER (Title)

ST. PETER PORT (Name of Parish)

Identity Card issued by (Official issuing Identity Card to insert his initials.)

STAR TYP., BORDAGE—00M/10/1940.

Islanders had to fill in forms such as this.
(Details of dad's on page 141).

11

The Islanders felt the Island was governed well under the very difficult circumstances, one would have had to have actually lived through the five years here to understand the feeling of being surrounded by so many. Here we were trapped on an Island approximately 25 square miles (6 x 4) and overtaken by thousands. At times the Germans numbered and almost equalled again our population of approximately 20,000; 1 to 1 Islander! Literally surrounded in every way, what could our Officials do in these circumstances? It's so easy for some 'reporters' to write now and some articles that have been printed of late have angered and upset many of the 'older' Islanders who stayed behind and who remember so much better than I do. Really having received quite a few telephone calls from 'newspapers' (apart from wanting facts about the Jewish ladies) *some* only wanted to report 'sensationalism'.

There were other Islanders who punched and struck the Germans and were severely punished in prisons. Another brave Guernseyman Mr. Roy Machon, a projector operator at the Regal Cinema, started converting English silver coins into 'V' sign brooches which featured the King's head inside a 'V'. Hundreds of these were made and worn on the reverse side of the coat lapel, but eventually the Germans caught up with him and he was tried and sentenced to six months imprisonment to be served at a Munich prison, which he did so; then after was sent also to the Laufen Internment Camp where many of the 1,000 or so Islanders and Sarkees were also sent at this time because they were English-born or had English connections, or were just troublemakers and who had offended against Occupation Laws. The majority were deported to Biberach but other camps included Dorsten, Compiegne, Kreutzberg, Liebenau, Wurzach, and of course Laufen where Ron and Roy met up and became friends.

Another young Guernseyman escaped the net and carried on making brooches on a reduced scale — out of sixpences, shillings, florins and half crowns. He was lucky not to get caught.

Because we had no radio sets, five brave men decided to form an underground organisation who made it their business to circulate the BBC news around the Island. This daily news sheet printed for almost two years (May 1942 to February 1944), was known as GUNS (Guernsey's Underground News Service) — was handed to trusted friends but unfortunately must have eventually got into the wrong hands and these men were reported to the Gestapo with serious consequences. 'GUNS' being conceived by Mr Charles Machon, sadly died in Hameln-Weser Hospital on October 26, 1944 after being transferred from Potsdam Prison. The other four men concerned were also sentenced and were at Frankfurt prison for two months then were transferred to the much grimmer prison at Naumburg, south of Leipzig.

To be fair, if one behaved himself 'they' (on the whole) did not interfere — they would annoy and want to frighten one especially when merry with a drink or two (remember with mum in 'A Child's War'?) When civilians did not obey or tow the line, families would suffer. Also new laws would be introduced and everyone would be punished. The German authorities would also carry out a very harsh punishment on their own members of the German Army if caught out of line. They thought themselves a disciplined and 'correct' army and obeyed orders from the 'top dogs' to whoever deserved punishment, Islanders or fellow Germans.

THERE WERE VAYS AND MEANS EH?

Despite the seriousness of the times, there were many lighter moments, especially when one can look back. I can well remember my mother and father telling many funny stories especially to visitors after the War was over. Many evenings were spent laughing — but then that was mum and dad always looking on the bright side and seeing the funny side of life.

I have mentioned in my early schooldays being at Vauvert School where the Germans soon stored their stock of flour in the upstairs classrooms. Well, many of the boys seemed to have weak bladders and had the need to visit the toilet frequently, but taking paper bags in their pockets would each time (although out of bounds) help themselves to bags of flour! We girls were too slow it seemed on that one — and I wonder now whether the teachers knew and closed their eyes to it.

Another little story of a boy (my age) who wanted to relieve himself did so in a German boot! He was with friends on the Coast Road and noticing the Germans swimming and their clothes near the slip — thought he'd leave his mark and then run like mad. True tale, as I spoke to this Guernseyman during the summer at the 'Olde Market'. Boys will be boys eh? But at least he had his own back for not being allowed to swim also.

These little stories gladly never came to light and there are probably hundreds more, just little acts by youngsters and grown-ups alike to try and get even.

During the very grim and really boring days (and years!) for the adults, the population relied on the daily local newspapers for news. With the increasing shortage of paper (the daily consisted of one sheet only) it consisted mostly of German propaganda and just local general information for everyone, rationing etc. not forgetting the LAWS AND ORDERS! by order of the Kommandant.

On the back page, there were many columns of 'Wanted' or 'Sale or Exchange' — it was amazing what people wanted to give in exchange, mainly for food or a packet of tea. I noted even Mr. J. Glide (a chimney sweep on the Island) was asking and was desperate for soap. Just none to be had. At times there was a ration of hard, gritty and non-lather blocks from France but what folks would give for a bar of Lifebuoy — sheer luxury!

Other newspapers I came across and there were several ladies urgently desperate for babies' teats, even after our Liberation too. Apart from mum's own, what possibly could be used in place of them I wonder? It set me thinking as babies were being born and some mothers just could not accommodate.

Islanders did not advertise when cats went missing — they knew their pets had been either eaten by the foreign prisoners working here or during the later period, the Germans. There were no cats left in the Island at the end and Germans were also known to eat the hedgehogs! They were also eating their large magnificent horses and any dogs they managed to find or steal. They were literally starving at this time, and naturally stole cattle too from farmers. Stealing all through the years was rife islandwide, especially in the country parishes. On December 29th 1944 it was reported in the Evening Press that locals were accused and brought to court for stealing a heifer (one stolen even on Christmas Day!) another local caught stealing a pig, others had stolen a quantity of carrots from a house (too many robberies of this kind said the magistrate – sentence – 14 days hard labour!) another case of a man stealing tobacco leaves from a greenhouse and more carrots (likewise – 7 days hard labour), also likely to see on the local paper a 'cow was missing' (November 1943) — very quickly to be found on tables I'm sure and sometimes on the owner's table too as they would want the news to get around a cow had been stolen — a lie, but the record had to be kept straight! There were vays and means eh? to beat the enemy!

WAS 'BULLNECK' THE DREADED 'OTTO'?

At times during 1940–1945 so many people were hungry and apparently there was a continued outbreak of diarrhoea and vomiting. (Even as early as the winter of 1941–1942). This account brought to mind 'our' potato game we children used to get up to. This very early period was probably the time when sister Joyce and I helped with the shortage at home. Joyce not yet 9 years old and myself not yet 11! The exact ages of our older grandchildren Ryan and Carly — looking at them now it doesn't seem possible that we had to scrounge for anything at that early age and mum and dad must have worried for us at the time. A bit of fun for us though, we didn't seem to worry, or I don't remember us being bothered about our visiting. It is with interest I've heard a friend Alf Le Poidevin talk of a cruel O.T. (a Nazi who was of the T.O.D.T. organisation) and who frequently bullied prisoners and locals alike at the Harbour. Alf worked for the States Public Works and with permits, he and others in the course of their work had to have dealings with the Germans. I knew 'Otto' worked between the Harbour (White Rock) and the Truchot seeing to their food stocks arriving in the Island. On one occasion this feared and hated bully known to all the workers down there as 'Bullneck' (obviously because of his size!) thrust a revolver into Alf's chest because he decided to go against his order — Alf soon changed his mind, naturally! I feel sure this 'BULLNECK' by Alf's description was the big bully and infamous 'OTTO' we also had to put up with at our potato collecting and the one who gave me the boot!

It appears that for Christmas 1941 everyone had a *2lb ration* of potatoes then *no more* on ration until the *end of April 1942* when the first signs of a ration came — 1lb. per head! In between times the Germans promised a ration but they collected them instead and took them all (probably to their 'Truchot' Food Stores where we were busily engaged!) At the vegetable market potato skins were selling at 2d. a lb! Can you wonder why Mum and Dad did not mind us scrounging around (like she also had to do) to feed our family of 9? Around this time there also came a first ration of sugar after seven weeks without. The first winter months under occupation certainly proved to be a 'hunger period' for many. Recipes printed in the Guernsey Press were appreciated such as 'Limpet Pie' and 'Parsnip honey', ugh!

It just so happens that only last week I was talking to a holiday-maker who had worked on the mainland since the war with a Guernsey and Jersey man. They had both lived on the Islands as children during the war years and both had died in their early 50s. He wondered whether their early deaths were due to the shortages and vitamin deficiences endured then. I could only answer that looking at my school photograph and knowing so many pupils, many had *died* young. I don't know but maybe this could be a reason and it makes one think when asked questions such as this.

RED CROSS MESSAGES AND
H.M.S. CHARYBDIS

On a happier note, it was also interesting for my parents and others to read the messages that had been received by locals from their loved ones on the mainland. These messages were sent through the Red Cross Society and were printed in the newspapers for all to read.

There was usually a long wait of five or six months for these messages to come through and then answered. The senders had to keep to twenty five words or under and that usually proved difficult. So much to say and so much news was wanted in return but every letter naturally had to be censored. Strictly personal news only was permitted in the message and its reply, but islanders sometimes managed to get strange and coded messages through — especially where Jerry and the Jerries were concerned.

A clever and well-thought message also arrived from the Headmaster of Torteval School who had evacuated to England — "Tommy, Joe and Sam's boys working very hard. Doing very good work. Should graduate with honours near future." People who knew Torteval well and who had dear children under the Headmaster's care knew no-one of these names. Of course after thought it came to them — *Joseph* Stalin, Uncle *Sam* in the USA meant the same as John Bull in Britain and then *Tommy* — the British soldier!!

More personal and like most of the messages that came through was similar to one sent to my mother from an aunt. Her husband (my uncle Ted) was one of three uncles living with us during the Occupation, also their son Teddy. The Red Cross did a wonderful job and everyone was so grateful to them for their truly wonderful service. The messages were a great morale booster to families here and to their loved ones, the refugees away.

Other messages received were not of good news. You may recall in 'A Child's War' and remember me mentioning a sailor, Guernseyman Rex Holloway who was killed in action.

Many, many more relations and friends of loved ones lost and killed in the War must have dreaded receiving letters such as this. Guernsey experienced a very sad and moving ceremony when nineteen seamen were buried at the Foulon Cemetery on November 17th, 1943. H.M.S. Charybdis a light cruiser, was leading six destroyers, but received a direct hit by German E boats with a loss of 462 lives on the night of 23rd/24th October. Nineteen bodies were washed up on our shores, another twenty-three on other islands and France. Many hundreds, probably thousands, of people from all walks of life attended and paid

Deutsches Rotes Kreuz

Präsidium / Auslandsdienst
Berlin SW 61, Blücherplatz 2

R.O.B. GUERN
3015

ANTRAG

an die Agence Centrale des Prisonniers de Guerre
— Internationales Komitee vom Roten Kreuz —
auf Nachrichtenvermittlung

REQUÊTE

de la Croix-Rouge Allemande, Présidence, Service Étranger
à l'Agence Centrale des Prisonniers de Guerre, Genève
— Comité International de la Croix-Rouge —
concernant la correspondance

bittet, an
prie de bien vouloir faire parvenir à

1. Absender Mrs. G. Finigan, 30 Canigers,
   Expéditeur GUERNSEY. C.I.

2. Empfänger Mrs. Edward Finigan, c/o A.C.B.751,
   Destinataire Gaddun House, Queen Street, MANCHESTER 2
   ENGLAND.

folgendes zu übermitteln / ce qui suit:

(Höchstzahl 25 Worte!)
(25 mots au plus!)

Dearest Kath and children,
We are well well. Hope you're same.
Longing to see you. Don't worry.

Love, Glad, Bill, children.

(Datum / Date) 12-9-42

4 DEC. 1942

PASSED P.162

3. Empfänger antwortet umseitig
   Destinataire répond au verso

(Unterschrift / Signature)
Gladys Finigan

4861... 5 MAR 1943

---

4. Antwort des Empfängers :
   Réponse du destinataire :

(Höchstzahl 25 Worte!)
(25 mots au plus!)

DEAR GLADYS
PLEASE TO KNOW THAT ALL
KEEPING WELL HOPE YOU HAVE
GOT TED, TEDDY STILL WITH YOU
BOBBY GETTING quite BIG BOY
LOVE KATH

(Datum / Date) 20·1·43

(Unterschrift)
(Signature)

PASSED P.172

COMITÉ INTERNATIONAL DE LA CROIX-ROUGE · GENÈVE

their last respects, a wonderful display of wreaths and floral tributes were laid. German forces and German marines were also present and laid wreaths but seeing such a large crowd of Islanders who attended, the Germans put a stop to all future demonstrations at funerals. To the present time, there is still a service held at the Foulon Cemetery every year, remembering the seamen laid to rest, and survivors make the effort from the mainland to join in the ceremony. One particular survivor made several Guernsey friends (including us) during his visits here and who really lived all his life for the Navy, but has died recently. Sadly we shall receive no more letters or cards with the signature 'Capt David Royle' which he always signed himself as, although not the Captain of the H.M.S. Charybdis.

Outside news that helped to keep the adults going and even the children, were the leaflets which were dropped by Allied aircraft to help the population know the true facts of the war. This particular one was dropped during September 1940 with a message on the front for the Islands.

Everyone was so grateful for any contact with the outside world, the adults did not want to be forgotten at any time. There were definitely times when we did wonder if Britain had totally forgotten us. Of course the grown-ups (maybe a few?) had no knowledge of the several landings and commando raids that took place on the beaches into the Island from 1940 onwards. Together with information given by islanders who managed to escape to the mainland and telling of our heavy fortifications etc. around the Island, the authorities probably thought and knew it would be unwise to try and recapture the Islands. Looking back now they were right.

CURRENCY AND CLAIMS

Local letters and accounts etc. were posted and delivered throughout the Island but as early as January 1941 the stock of penny ones were exhausted, then the twopenny stamps were allowed to be cut diagonally and used temporarily until local penny ones were printed. A Guernsey newspaper man designed the new stamps and the first day of issue was for the 1d. Red — February 18, 1941, ½d. Green — April 7, 1941; 2½d. Blue — April 12, 1944. In all 4,667,500 were printed on the Island. Apparently the Guernsey stamps were eagerly bought by the German stamp collectors. There would have been a greater short supply of suitable paper had the German Commandant not made the Order that no-one might buy more than ten stamps at a time. Like everything else, envelopes ran out also and my father when sending out

News from England

SEPTEMBER 1940   DISTRIBUTED BY THE R.A.F.   No. 1

A MESSAGE FROM HIS MAJESTY THE KING

The Queen and I desire to convey to you our heartfelt sympathy in the trials which you are now enduring. We earnestly pray for your speedy liberation, knowing that it will surely come.

GEORGE R.I.

TO THE CHANNEL-ISLANDERS

All of you, His Majesty's loyal subjects on the Channel Islands, must keep asking yourselves two great questions:—"How long must we put up with the German occupation?", and "How are our friends on the mainland?", and This news-sheet brings you the heartening answers. We on the mainland are in good heart. By subjecting our women and children to the wickedest form of warfare known to history, Hitler has only stiffened our backs. And the events of the last three weeks have only served to confirm Mr. Churchill's words of August 21st, that "the road to victory may not be so long as we expect." Nor may the day be so distant when we shall come to your relief. All our rapidly and enormously increasing strength is directed towards that day. When the shadow of the bully will be lifted from you and from the whole of Europe. We shall continue to bring you the news from England as often and as regularly as we can.

British planes made two raids on the night Sept. 23rd/24th doing considerable damage and dropping copies of these leaflets in many parts of the Island. Scenes at 'Vazon' race-course where due to lack of wind most of them fell , saw many German soldiers busily employed at an early hour collecting, (even climbing trees) and frequently obliged to run brandishing their revolvers and bayonets chasing the locals (also children!!) who were more than eager to find the leaflets.

Two days later a notice was published threatening 15 years imprisonment if these leaflets were handed on, or contents circulated, and anyone in possession of this 'enemy propaganda' must deliver them to the Feldkommandantur, Grange Lodge Hotel, 25th September 1940, but I doubt if any were handed in!

NEWS FROM ENGLAND

ESCAPE FROM GUERNSEY

Eight Reach Britain

London, September 27

A PARTY of eight men have successfully escaped from Guernsey to England in a 20 ft. boat. The London press is headlining their adventures.

They left Guernsey under cover of darkness and rowed half a mile before using the motor. When they were about two miles out four flares were dropped by three German planes flying over them. One fell only twenty yards from the boat, but they were not seen.

Just after passing the Caskets their engine broke down, but the repairs were finished in four hours and they eventually sighted Start Point, the landmark for which they were making.

The party consisted of Mr. Frederick Hockey, 47, a signalman employed by the harbour administration at St. Peter port, three of his sons, Frederick, 25, George, 21, and Harold 16, who were engaged in tomato growing, and Messrs. William Mahy, Percy de Port, William Dorey and Herbert Bichard, independent growers.

These pictures portray the solemn scene at the burial of the bluejackets.

The Dean of Guernsey is seen passing from grave to grave, each enclosing one coffin, with breastplate, to pronounce the final words of Benediction; and the other photograph shows only a small section of the wonderful tribute of wreaths.

WEDNESDAY, NOVEMBER 17th, 1943.

A moving service when seamen from HMS Charybdis were laid to rest with German forces and German marines present. They also laid wreaths at the ceremony.

21

accounts had to re-use envelopes by crossing out original addresses. Nothing was wasted.

Regarding currency, at the beginning of the Occupation, we were using Guernsey money including English money and coinage. Because the 'visiting uninvited guests' decided to hoard and keep the silver coins as souvenirs, there became a shortage of the smaller currency. A lot of locals also decided to hide away extra English and Guernsey money in case 'Liberation came quickly' or perhaps a chance would come their way to escape and find freedom. Anyway, because of the shortage of coins, the Island had to produce more notes — 6d, 1/-, 2/- etc., also having the German Reichmarks and pfennigs etc at the same time. Towards the end of 1943, all the Guernsey and British paper money was called in and the Reichmarks became the official currency until our Liberation. I can remember a lot of people wondering whether the German money would be honoured, but it was of course at the end of the war with great relief to the Black marketeers I'm sure!

Food and commodities throughout was only to be sold at a controlled price (given by the States) and should perhaps the growers, farmers or the market stalls charge a penny more, the people concerned were brought to court with many such cases coming to light. The same being for the few caught Blackmarketeers, but *after* Liberation no particular action was taken, nor against the informers who wrote to the German Authorities anonymously. Many islanders felt it was jealously that drove individuals to write and although nothing came to light after, probably many hoped they were punished in some way by their immediate family who were disgraced by their deeds and actions. Afterwards the handling or thoughts of any 'action' or prosecution would have been in the hands of the British Military. (Local Authorities informed 'The Star' newspaper October, 1945).

Although dad apparently was not a great scholar, he did very well after being a gunner (see further on) and he learned his trade and worked in the building department of the States of Guernsey, his trade being mainly a plasterer. Whilst working for the States, he fell from the inside roof of the vegetable market but fortunately was not seriously injured. With the height, he could easily have been killed.

Then with confidence, he started out on his own, knowing most of the trade he worked as always very hard and got on well. Of course, during the Occupation with no lorry and materials in very short supply, it was a case of making do with anything he could get and everywhere he went with materials were on hand trucks. Not very easy with our Guernsey hills. He had a good head for business and his customers kept with him for many years — he gained a lot of respect from them. He treated them all very fair, did a good job and they were friends. He was a gentleman from the 'Old School' — always touching his cap on greeting, either 'Good morning Ma'am' or 'Sir', and always with great respect for others.

Not so friendly were the Occupying Forces, neither did they respect dad's belongings. At the time of the Occupation, the brothers Bill and Ted (dad and uncle) worked together as 'Finigan Bros' and they owned two cottages in the Water Lanes, Rosina Cottage and Brook Cottage.

The German forces had occupied these cottages like so many other properties. Families had left their homes so quickly and as they were, with food, furniture etc. at the time of the evacuation in June 1940. In a very short time families had to decide whether to stay or leave — four days of confusion and near panic especially for the parents of young children. It must have been so difficult for everyone to decide to leave their homes and a worrying task for the authorities to organise shipping in such a short while. Approximately 20,000 islanders left their only belongings — everything they owned even to pets, it was a case of now or never, and when empty of families the Germans just walked in and took over.

In other cases some German Officers were billeted with civilians, usually with middle-aged or elderly widows. Like my aunt, Mrs Winnie Salmon my father's sister who was living in a large house and with having large rooms took in lodgers. My two uncles who had also gone to live with aunty Win when their wives and children evacuated, eventually after a while had to move out because of these new unwelcome 'lodgers'. Incidently aunty Win had four children (two sets of twins) and three evacuated with the school from Guernsey – Rosemary, Raymond and Joan, John was also at boarding school on the mainland at the time – so now it was the case of having to put up with 'others' and one can only imagine how low she felt at the time. She had to keep their rooms clean and in return my aunt occasionally gained a little in the way of food, apparently they never handed the little treats directly to her, they just left them indoors for her to find. She hardly ever saw them but certainly heard their comings and goings – and my gran did too! And in return my gran (dad and aunty Win's mum – Emma Brassel who also lived at 'Shaftesbury House') was overheard more than once!! Eric Sirett who at the time of 1941/42 was also living at my aunt's and heard my gran every time remark when hearing their 'boots' on the path – 'oh dear, there's the 'B.......'' Germans again!' (Quite out of character I would say, as gran lived to almost 90 years of age, I remember her well and never from her did I hear even a little swear word.) Well one day there was a knock at aunty Win's living room door and she called 'who's there?' – back came the direct answer 'its the 'ploody' Germans again!!!' As Eric recalled, although all taken aback with the reply and they were worried for the minute but to the German's credit (his mother was an American lady and he spoke perfect English) he certainly showed a sense of humour at the time, but he also told Aunty Win to warn gran to be very careful as to what she said in the future. Now looking back like Eric says – very funny especially remembering and thinking of Granny Brassel, as during her later life was a quiet and gentle lady. Aunty Win had mentioned later and often said they treated her well and they were gentlemen; she was probably lucky to have clicked with the ones she had billeted on her, but there were others!! Many people who had spent many years, maybe all their lives in the same house had been forced to leave and in most cases with very short notice.

Going back to dad's properties, the German forces had occupied both the cottages and both were badly damaged and many fittings removed. Owners were told to claim for expenses and loss and printed here is a letter to the States Supervisor dated 8th July 1945 claiming for these damages after the war had ended. Like everyone else who had Germans living solely in properties, no financial gain or rent for the whole five years was given to the owners. Many properties were left in a very bad state of repair, gardens overgrown and neglected also in most, left in a filthy condition. I am sure that was to be expected after probably quite a number of different Germans had been living in these homes, then moving on, just coming and going between 1940 and 1945. Dad was claiming £176.10.0d, for the cottages needed complete decoration. The bath had been removed and was missing also; and so had to be replaced. Also included in this claim was damage caused by practice gun fire behind our home 'Rose Villa' at Les Canichers. The four guns were 'French harbour guns' with a range of six and a half miles and they were situated at Les Cotils (or the Blue Mountains as we call them). When Germans practised their gun-fire, the noise was shattering and we had to vacate our homes. This usually happened at first daylight. So close were we to the gun fire that plaster fell from the ceiling in the top bedrooms and these all needed a lot of attention. For a while, my uncle and the friend staying (also my cousin) had to move out. The roof also needed repairing with slates off caused by the vibrations.

Eventually with much correspondence to the States offices and the War Damage Department, dad was awarded £78.00 in total which he received in 1947. This amount also included his Dodge lorry. It had been apparently purchased by dad during 1932 costing £265.00. The Germans requisitioned it in February 1942 and dad received at the time, a 'generous' £2 from the States of Guernsey! This amount was later deducted in 1947 from the total allowance on the lorry of £20.

People and families who decided to remain on the mainland after liberation lost everything and received no grants — nothing either for owners of property which the States felt was too badly damaged and

Claims

30, CANICHERS, GUERNSEY.

.................8th July................1945.

Mr. Marquand, States Supervisor, States Office, Guernsey.

DR. TO **W. FINIGAN**

BUILDING AND JOBBING CONTRACTOR.

ESTIMATES FREE.   **PERSONAL AND PROMPT ATTENTION.**

Star Typ.

Billeting Officer, States Office.

Dear Sir,

    I beg to notify you that I have taken back into my control, my property known as 'Rosina Cottage' situated in the Water Lanes St. Peter Port.

    This property has been under German control since October 9th 1941.

    I should like to bring to your notice, the following damage caused through the German occupation of the said property, also missing articles.

    Cupboard doors missing also shelves.

    Wooden partitions, bath. Wash hand basin damaged.

    Locks missing. Floors damaged and windows broken.

    Hoping you will keep this report for future reference.

    I remain,

    Yours obediently,

W. Finigan

German forces and prisoners of war did not live in 'Barracks' or 'Special' areas. They lived in homes and hotels all over the island amongst the islanders.

Channel Islands (Property) Rehabilitation Scheme.
———————————— GUERNSEY. ————————————

Applicant's Name and Address
W.J. FINIGAN,
  30. Canichers,
      St. Peter Port.
Business or Occupation
Builder.

Situation of Property damaged or lost
30. Canichers, Rosina and Brook
Cottages, Water Lanes,
St. Peter Port.
Brief description
Dwelling house and 2 cottages damaged
by German troops during the Occupation.

Salvage
To Claimant and incorporated in
Assessment.

APPROVAL (for official use only).

S. of G. Housing Authority

.............C IA.............Member of Committee.

...............6|8|46....Date

B. of T. (C.I.)

..............................:.......Executive Officer

...................7|8|46...........Date

B. of T. (London)

....
..................................Date

Home Office.

....
..................................Date

SUMMARY OF ASSESSMENT:—

Amount:—	APPLIED FOR	VALUE 1939	PRESENT DAY PRICE LEVEL	MINIMUM AMOUNT ON A UTILITY BASIS ESSENTIAL FOR REHABILITATION
(a) Land and Buildings.	142 10 0		60 0 0	60 0 0
Land as distinct from Buildings.				
(b) Business Equipment.	35 0 0		18 0 0	18 0 0
(c) Stocks in Trade.				
(d) Private Chattels.				
TOTAL	177 10 0		78 0 0	78 0 0
Less Amounts received from any source. for Motor Vehicle	2 0 0		- - -	- - -
£	175 10 0		78 0 0	78 0 0

Assessor's
  Fees   £3 3s. 0d.

Date   8th August, 1946.

Signature p.p. HUGH V. ALLEN & CO.

Full Report and Schedules, see over and attached.

Star Typ., Bordage.

I'm sure Dad's claim for damage was small compared to most (August 1946) too expensive to make habitable again. There were many of these beyond repair being almost wrecked with all wood gone (doors, beams etc., taken for warmth and cooking) and fittings taken (also furniture of course). Houses were ransacked and anything of value was taken and sent to homes in Germany too. Corrugated roofs were also ripped apart by the German Forces to be used for covering etc. for their own war defences. No grants were given towards considered luxury items — such as wireless sets, which were damaged and unusable after being called in, cameras, nor for guns, rifles, etc.

Although dad received a grant for his lorry, none was forthcoming towards private motor cars, motor cycles and bicycles, yachts and boats, nor buildings used as summer residences, summer houses, boundary walls and gates (a lot went missing!) and private garages. The amount of £2,500,000 which was voted by the British Government and administered by the States of Guernsey was purely to help the rehabilitation of families with basic needs. Although a generous amount, claims by Guernsey residents was very much greater than this. £6,000,000 in all was the sum granted and given to the Channel Islands.

Back to dad and I know he missed using his lorry very much. He worked hard and used hand trucks later, and all through the Occupation from 1942 I am sure as time went by, the Guernsey hills must have seemed steeper than ever before.

Also, I remember reading about poor Mr. Reuben Le Page's horses. Not only did he find the hills getting steeper as time went by, but he also could not understand why he had to pull the cart from the other side of the road! Yes, all traffic was made to travel on the right, which I am sure must have caused confusion at the beginning for everyone.

Although of late Guernsey has seen more road signs, still visitors complain of the few directions we have posted. During the war years I remember very well the many road signs in German for the benefit of the many military vehicles of all kinds, German motor bikes and horse pulled wagons. Can you imagine (by July 1941), Guernsey having only just under 50 private and commercial vehicles on the roads? Apart from these which were considered essential, there were locals using hundreds of bicycles. The Germans even called in bicycles for their own use. They wanted 100, but after a week only five had been handed in and they were old crocks at that. So then a compulsory order was made and naturally had to be obeyed! They got their 100, then they promptly wanted another 300, always wanting more from the locals it seemed! It was amazing where the others all came from even after this call in, many came to light — they really were a Godsend for school children at our school who had to travel daily from the country. On every bicycle was a box, perhaps an 'old' chip basket or bag always ready to accept 'anything' that was going. In the town everyone seemed to be pushing little 'carts', basket and walking stick push carts, — boxes or anything on wheels or prams (even dolls' prams) like our mum used to use daily — not for babies but to have just in case an extra vegetable could be had, one never refused to queue should food be on a stall and very handy to take for the daily trek to the bakehouse — called the 'Bakehouse Trot' by everyone. Feeding six hefty males and we children was never easy for mum.

'EVEN THOUGH'

So much has been written of our Occupation, many more tales I'm sure to come — for myself I promise not to say more. An Epilogue was written for the Guernsey Evening Press, May 9th 1945 and I think it says all.

Even though we have experienced a few air-raids; even though we've seen streets of shattered shop fronts and some homes blasted and ruined; even though two old couples and a grower were murdered by the Germans and a few others met violent deaths; even though our crops have been pillaged and plundered and our cattle filched from us; even though many of our fellows have suffered at the hand of the Gestapo and been flung into gaol; even though we saw many loved ones torn away and transported to internment camps at Biberach and Laufen; even though, for months, we have hovered on the very borderland of starvation; even though we have seen the matchless beauties of our coast and countryside gashed and scarred and disfigured for a decade by hideous fortifications; and even though property everywhere has been wrecked and furniture stolen; even remembering all these things, and many more which we have witnessed under the trampling heel of the Nazis, we must still admit that we have been the most fortunate people in all Europe.

Unlike the European peoples — and our own people in England — we have not had to cower in cellars for night after night awaiting a cataclysm from the skies. We have slept comfortably in our beds tranquil and undisturbed, for years on end.

Guernsey's freedom once again. May 9th 1945

CHAPTER 3

LIBERATION WITH LOVE,
LIFE & LAUGHTER

WAR BEGAN SUNDAY SEPTEMBER 3rd 1939
ENDED MAY 7th 1945 (surrender of Germany to Gt. Britain, U.S.A.
& Soviet Russia)
GUERNSEY OCCUPIED 30th JUNE 1940. MAY 8th 1945
MR. WINSTON CHURCHILL BROADCASTS "OUR DEAR
CHANNEL ISLANDS TO BE FREED TODAY"

There were many happy faces in and around our Town on the Monday and Tuesday, feeling an air of expectancy of freedom to come soon and our Liberation Day on Wednesday May 9th 1945 was just wonderful and I make no apologies for talking of it once more. One cannot forget this great day when really Guernsey went mad! How excited and happy everyone felt and so thankful at last to be free after five years of worry, tension, boredom and near starvation, especially during the latter part and past few months. Also, the threat always of being surrounded by so many of the enemy. It seems strange thinking back that really just a handful of British who freed us were amongst the German Garrison of thousands.

The Allied Liberation fleet anchored off St. Peter Port, May 8th and the surrender of the German forces occupying the Channel Islands was signed on board H.M.S. Bulldog on May 9th.

The excitement began early morning when two Guernseymen arrived with the first small group of troops. There was Lieutenant R. E. Ferbrache a Naval man and the other, Sergeant H. J. Hamon, who over the years was a great friend of my father's from before the War and whom I got to know very well since this time. They led the first small group of 22 troops on the morning of May 9th very proudly from the boat to the Weighbridge and then through the town and Esplanade, being mobbed, cuddled and kissed all the way — with many tears also from them and everyone in sight. I remember so well the chocolate, fruit, cigarettes and biscuits being handed out also being thrown from windows along the Esplanade. What fun we children had, really everyone did, including the Troops, they also had a wonderful time sharing in our Freedom. All the great excitement was really on the day of May 9th as many more Troops were to come ashore later during the day — everyone seemed to be crowded in the Town — happy with not a care in the world — just laughter, tears, hugging and singing. Yes I remember very well everyone singing with hand loud speakers placed all over the town. Approx 3,000 more troops were to arrive at the weekend, also many types of boats, even American amongst the convoy of almost 60 ships. Many vehicles and equipment etc. were being unloaded in the then 'Old Harbour'. We had sea planes flying overhead and also the sound of a wonderful British military band. This added so much to the celebrations and they stayed on in the Island playing at different venues for quite a while.

Scenes of our Liberation was naturally broadcast and this brought much excitement and relief to the many Islanders on the mainland who at last could hear what was happening on the Island. To know we were free at last brought much thanksgiving and then also celebrations amongst them. Quite soon after some Islanders were sending messages to their loved ones and they were touching to listen to on the Radio. Guernsey and the Channel Islands were certainly in the news at long last.

There were reports on the English newspapers, and one heading boldly printed 'LONDONER (Bowler and Umbrella) GOES TO GUERNSEY' reminded me of this little story. It was a strange sight for us on May 12th to witness this 'special' visitor. The loudest cheer of the day when the main British force arrived was not for the thousands of soldiers, but it was for the Londoner who walked up from the first assault craft firmly holding his bowler on his head with his left hand, clutching his tightly rolled umbrella wih his right and a despatch case tucked under his right arm. Mr C. D. Bickmore, a civil servant was carrying important plans for the complete rehabilitation of the Island, but it was the sight of this man complete with umbrella and bowler hat that brought tears and laughter and the singing of 'There'll always be an England'.

Behind the cheers and flag waving some families felt a tragic loss and shock as three people collapsed in Guernsey under the emotion of Liberation and died — also in Jersey two women died in the packed streets. Others weakened died too, one Guernsey lady was determined to walk the three miles to the Esplanade wanting just to shake hands with a British soldier and never arrived back home. She collapsed and died a few hours later.

On the Saturday of Liberation Week, it was to become a 'C' Day. Ceremony and Celebration but also for the days ahead that were being planned a feeling of 'carnival'. There were to be special weeks of nightly entertainment all over the Island. The main organiser of these events was Mr Alan Jory and in no time at all he was organising dances, especially so the open air ones at the Candie Auditorium where it was reported 2,000 people were admitted and never had the audience dropped to under 1,000! There were Whist Drives, Euchre Drives etc., Variety Shows and these dances were particularly held at the Royal Hotel when the forces brought in the 'Hokey Kokey' and we in turn exported I'm sure our 'Sarnia Cherie'!

NOW THE GOOD LIFE

First and foremost, food was promised for this weekend, also fuel, clothing and footwear. Enough food was to be brought over to keep the Islanders going for a fortnight, then within another seven days another two weeks supply would be arriving. These goods and the large number of troops were landed at L'Ancresse Bay. Little luxuries like chocolate, cigarettes and tobacco would come within a fortnight.

A luxury that did arrive again on 'C Day' was the national newspapers — the first in five years! Large advertising soon appeared in our newspapers 'Place your orders now for speedy service'. To the grown-ups there was a lot of catching up to do. The following first Sunday was to be Guernsey's 'Thanksgiving' Day, and was quietly spent at Church Services, when most Churches were packed.

Luxuries (yes!) like coal was expected to arrive and gas was to be available again in four to five weeks' time. None to be had since before Christmas 1944 — Mothers all over the Island must have been very relieved and excited too over this to have thoughts of heating for cooking and to have water during the day for longer than two hours and to have hot water too! It had been a very cold, dark and difficult winter. Rations were to be raised to $1\frac{1}{2}$ lb potatoes, 6oz flour, 4oz butter and 6oz sugar. All foods would gradually and slowly come into the Island. To add to all the excitement, up-to-date films were to be shown at the Regal Cinema, Upland Road. The first being 'The Working Man' featuring George Arliss followed by a cartoon film of 'Mickey Mouse' being first shown May 10th. Many Islanders queued at long last to watch together with a total British audience and to sing their hearts out. Being the first time in five years everyone was allowed to raise their voices in hearty patriotic songs with Kennedy Bott at the Compton organ. One can imagine the great atmosphere and the volume

32

of 1,000 happy voices and I'm sure the audience (and myself) did not let Kennedy Bott down when he told them all to 'let themselves go!'

Whilst the Islanders were contented with everything around them of course there was much work to be carried out. As early as May 10th mine sweepers of the Royal Navy were busy clearing the seas surrounding the Island because of the extensive minefields. All day the ships could be seen moving up and down our coast with the many explosions from time to time. There were land mines around our coasts, ammunitions, weapons etc., to be rounded up. By November 8th reports in 'The Star' newspaper — 14,000 tons of ammunition had been dumped. There were also machine guns, anti-aircraft guns, field guns, mortars and flame-throwers, many lorries and wireless equipment, etc, etc, (not forgetting the vast fortifications of one kind or another and what to do about them). Besides clearing this lot the armed forces had to either restore to rightful owners or dispose of these many items being — 208 farm carts, 250 bicycles, 200 tons of scrap metal, 833 tons of kindling wood, 9,929 items of saddlery and like goods, 5,000 blankets, 5,733 items of furniture, 467 items of crockery and hardware, 6, 541 tools, 255 motor vehicles, 64 motor vehicle parts and 80 other assorted items. It was difficult for us to imagine just how much work had to be done. Over 1,000 German troops were left to clear the mess – to remove defences, much barbed wire everywhere and the mines etc. The other approximate 10,000 who were in the Island at the time of Liberation were sent off to the mainland to prisoner-of-war camps.

One of the very first things to be done was for the 'Reichskreditkassen' —the German money we had used to be called in. The States Officials wanted the circulation to be handed in as soon as possible and the Banks and other outlets opened their doors on May 9th, 10th and 11th. Apparently the Guernsey currency notes had been secretly designed by the Guernsey Press Co., printed, and all arrangements made beforehand unknown to the German Authorities, the number of 'Reichskreditkassen' notes in circulation were 5,772,498, by 16th May, 2,488,514 had been exchanged. Officials were prepared to exchange notes to the value of half million pounds. Everyone holding identity cards could on these three days exchange their German money for the new printed Guernsey notes at the rate of 2/- per Reichsmark, and to the maximum of £20 in value. Owing to limited supply of the new notes persons holding large sums of reichsmarks were requested to pay these into the credit of their bank and to draw only sufficient local notes to meet their current needs. The 10 and 5 pfg. German coins continued to circulate as legal tender at the rate of 2 $\frac{1}{2}^d$ and 1 $\frac{1}{2}^d$ respectively until further notice and did for a short while. Islanders were indeed eager and anxious to rid themselves

The new notes issued 1945

of their 'dirty old' marks, as the banks reported during the short 'exchange' time almost the entire circulation had been brought in.

'We can now post for England' — another heading May 8th — which meant so much to most. Letters could be posted, but until the British postage stamps were available, all correspondence had to be posted over the counter at the Head Post Office. No parcels could be accepted yet

THANKSGIVING ISLANDWIDE

During the afternoon of 'C' Day 12th May a Proclamation and an Official Ceremony was held at the Elizabeth College with many dignatories present. Brigadier A. E. Snow R.E., O.B.E., the Officer Commanding the Forces on the Island amongst other speeches read out the King's message to some 2,500 people gathered for this most important occasion.

The King's Message — read by Brigadier Snow:—

"To my most Loyal People in the Channel Islands, I send my heartfelt greetings. Ever since my Armed Forces had to be withdrawn, you have I know looked forward with the same confidence as I have to the time of deliverance, we have never divided in spirit. Our hopes and fears, anxieties and determination have been the same and we have been bound together by an unshakable conviction that the day would come when the islands, the oldest possession of the Crown, would be liberated from enemy occupation. That day has now come and with all my peoples, I cordially welcome you on your restoration and freedom and your rightful place with the free nations of the world. Channel Islanders in their thousands are fighting in my service for the cause of civilisation, with their traditional loyalty, courage and devotion, their task is now ended, yet but for you a new task begins at once — to rebuild the fortunes of your beautiful Islands, in anticipation of re-union with relatives, friends and neighbours who have been parted from you by the circumstances of war, in this task you can count on the fullest support of my Government. It is my desire that your ancient privileges and institutions should be maintained and that you should resume as soon as possible your accustomed system of Government. Meantime, the immediate situation requires that responsibility for the safety of the Islands and the well being of the inhabitants should rest upon the Commander of the Armed Forces stationed in the Islands. I feel confident that the Civil Authorities who have carried such a heavy burden during the past years, will gladly co-operate with him in maintaining good Government and securing the distribution of the supplies which he is bringing with him. It is my earnest hope that the Islands reinstated in their ancestral relationship to the Crown, will soon again regain their former happiness and prosperity.

Signed George VI

It was also at this time many thanksgiving services were being held on the Island and the Churches were well filled. Many collections were made for the British Red Cross as parcels were still being issued after our Liberation (six to each in all). We were all so thankful to the 'Vega' the relief ship that brought so much to us when badly needed. On her last trip the children received a 'special gift' of honey sent at the time by Her Royal Highness Princess Elizabeth. As a matter of interest the 'Vega' carried a total of 4,344 tons of Red Cross supplies to the Channel Islands which included 435,032 food parcels, 22,200 special invalid diet parcels, 500 cases of medical supplies, 23 tons of soap and 500,000 cigarettes. The total cost to the Red Cross and St. John was well over £250,000, a fortune in those days. Later on her sixth and final visit she brought Canadian parcels containing flour, sugar, yeast, biscuits, clothing, footwear, household and toilet soaps, salt, diesel oil, medical supplies and *our Honey*! At around the same time 'The Hymn of the Besieged' was written and composed by two 'Sarnians'. They had the hymn printed and made available to the public. Donations were given to the British Red Cross together with many more fund raising events that were to take place and in a very short while, to May 18th, donations to the Red Cross already amounted to £42,071 12. 4d.

'The Hymn of the Besieged'

Dark were the days we called in fear
'Help us oh Lord our cross to bear'
Beneath the Invaders heel we lay
Loved ones growing weaker every day

Hungry and cold we cried to Thee
Shut from the world across the sea
'Give us this day our daily Bread'
Waked each morning to hours of dread!

Ill Shod! Ill clad, both old and young
Nightly we called — 'oh Lord! How long?'
Searching for help, from sea and sky!
'Hear us Heavenly Father! Hear our cry!'

Forgive us Lord if we did doubt!
They loving presence — how we shout —
with gladdened hearts — forgive us Lord!
We were only human neath the sword!

Thou heards't our Prayers came the Glad Day!
Sent though the ship from far away!
Thou gavest Lord — our — Daily Bread!
Brought to us beneath the Cross-of-Red!

Now thank we Lord for all thy Love,
Dark days are over! Sun above —
Streams o'er world that cries to thee
Thanks to God on High, who makes us FREE!

It appears that a Dance Band musician Mr Charles Gardner also a composer of cheerful tunes during the Occupation for local shows awoke with a solemn tune in his head. With the help of Mr Ernest Tostevin a well known organist the Hymn was written and sung all over the Island at services, with a copy being sent to their majesties the King and Queen.

Maureen Des Caudevilles who was 16 years old and a friend of mine from the 'Occupation' Dancing School also wrote this poem in gratitude.

Thanks to the "Vega"

Now the time has arrived for the Vega's return,
This to be her last journey we recently learn,
Her help in the past, has been our mainstay
Our gratitude to her we can never repay.

The Vega has helped all, the old and the young,
The sick and the needy through months that were long
But now liberated in our thoughts she will stay
As the Vega who helped to make lighter our way.

Just a word for the Captain and crew who were brave,
To bring us the food in rough weather and waves,
Our thanks to them also we cannot express
When they came to our aid, we were in distress.

And last but not least we will hope for the day,
When the Vega will come without much delay

With her various cargoes, as in days of yore
And still we will thank her as never before.

(Proceeds again were given to the Red Cross)

Fund raising began after the 'Vega's' first visit and during the unloading of her second visit also £30,000 was raised, and sent to the Red Cross from the Islands, much fund raising continued for this worthwhile cause. Up to May 9th the Island collection in Jersey had also reached a great amount, £60,000.

CHAPTER 4

THEIR MAJESTIES ARRIVE 1945

On May 24th — it was reported that Brigadier A. E. Snow the Channel Islands Forces Commander told members of the States that 10,000 Germans had been removed and that over 1,000 would be left here to 'clear up the mess they had made'. The Brigadier also announced that 24 ships had discharged their cargoes in 10 days and at the moment there was a large cargo of oranges and 20 million cigarettes loaded at Southampton, ready to be dispatched for the Channel Islands. On arrival in early June a gift of 100 cigarettes was given to all grown ups who were in possession of identity cards.

At the States meeting the Bailiff warmly thanked Brigadier Snow, his officers and all his troops for the wonderful things they had done since arriving on the Island. 'It has been a miracle in the way everything has gone so smoothly and in the way they have brought food here'. Then Brigadier Snow gave some interesting facts by saying 9,000 tons of stores had been discharged, 5,000 tons for Guernsey and 4,000 going 'to another place'. There were cheers, clapping and stamping of feet when he announced the departure of the Germans, also the same number of 10,000 from 'the other place' and from Alderney 2,500. We were not sorry to see the back of them and I think this picture tells the story . . . (See next page)

'ISLAND ESCAPEE'S ENGLISH ENCOUNTER WITH GERMAN GUARD'. An interesting headline and to one gentleman a reversal of roles! A Guernsey fisherman escaped from Guernsey in August 1943 and who now had working under him one of the German guards who controlled his own movement before he managed to get away from Guernsey! He had written to his relatives 'when I was fishing in Guernsey I had to report daily to the German fishing guard. Two weeks ago I applied to the Authorities for 20 German prisoners to work at my factory clearing barbed wire. Who should be among them but the St. Sampson's fishing guard! He recognised me immediately and tried to make friends but I would have none of it and I saw to it

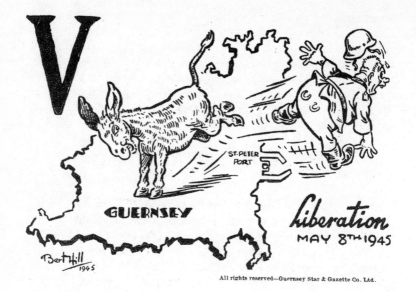

GUERNSEY

Liberation
MAY 8TH 1945

Bert Hill
1945

that he was kept hard at work. He was captured in France just after D-Day. It's a small world!' he concluded.

'Special Aid Calling' The Star newspaper *May 26th* Volunteers urgently wanted for darning socks for forces stationed in Guernsey! I noted in the same newspaper a three day holiday was to be given to the majority of the garrison on the Island. A well earned break I'm sure for those feet certainly needed a rest! They had and continued to work wonders for the Island.

You may remember me telling you of the welcome we gave and everyone on the Island did to these heroes of ours — several came to our home and we enjoyed their company and I'm sure they enjoyed mum and dad's too. We specially remember when 'Freddie Frinton' appeared in the 'Stars in Battledress' — (the concerts given at the time at the 'Central Hall') he would always shout from the stage — Hullo there 'Gladys', and 'Molly' and 'Joyce' Cooee! with a wave! Of course we felt proud and honoured to know him and for him to shout our names out in front of all those people, it was lovely for us youngsters.

Many friends were made and a large consignment of our 'Liberation' Boys stayed on for a further four to five months to see to it that our Island was shipshape once more — the last of the R.E.'s (200 strong) of FORCE 135 left on September 25th 1945. Young men who had stayed behind in the Island hoped perhaps to see something now of the outside world and to do something for their King and country in

40

return, and on *May 31st* 90 Sarnians volunteered for the Forces, by *June 5th* another 127 between the ages of 14 and 33.

Between the Islands of Guernsey, Jersey, Alderney and Sark more than 30,000 refugees had left for the mainland. Fully 8,000 to 10,000 being more than 10 per cent of the peace time population had served during the war years in the forces. Sadly 230 islanders had been killed or had died through their injuries. Many others had worked in war factories doing their bit towards the war effort — now the local boys wanted their turn.

Another great day for Guernsey was to be June 6th, 1945 and for us children as we were to meet the King and Queen! King George VI and Queen Elizabeth were to visit the Islands. Very poor weather conditions altered the plans so now they were to arrive on June 7th (my Father's 42nd birthday too! He must have been very happy and honoured by their visit on that birthday).

Flags were flying everywhere and everyone was out to greet Their Majesties. Strangely enough the German Guns gave the Royal Salute on their arrival and departure! Twenty one rounds of ammunition which had been made presumably by the Germans! Yes, some of the prisoners who were in the island clearing mines were put on making ammunition. They were asked whether they would be prepared to do it for the Royal Salute and apparently all said they would. Along the sea front at Les Banques the Russian soldiers who had worked and slaved on the Island were all lined up. Very smartly dressed and spick and span in brand new Khaki battle dress with U.S.S.R. proudly showing on their shoulders — all very happy to have places of Honour for this great occasion. Just past the 'Half Way' again on the Esplanade the French were also lined up and fitted out the same as the Russians, but proudly showing 'French' on their shoulders. Freedom also at last for them.

We school children had a place of Honour too and were all gathered at Candie Gardens enjoying a good view of the Royal party. Another week of Celebration was being organised in Honour of the King and Queen's visit, all proceeds again were given to the British Red Cross by Mr. Alan Jory and members of the Guernsey Entertainment Committee who did so much at this time.

A 'GIFT' WAS POISON

Afterwards the German prisoners left on the island were allowed to roam free in certain zones and apparently one war correspondent from a national newspaper (May 20th) was in Guernsey and when rounding a corner in a country lane was facing a prisoner on a motor bike — in that second he fully expected to be shot but to his surprise the German saluted and roared on, later two officers in a car did exactly the same!

There were many warnings to the Public not to purchase or accept goods from members of the German forces. Any person doing so was advised to report immediately to the police to avoid prosecution. There was also worry over children finding firearms, live ammunition and hand grenades. It was feared children were visiting billets where Germans formally had been stationed. (Also grown-ups looking for 'souvenirs'). At the same time a notice was printed regarding very dangerous and many varieties of drugs that had been left at hospitals, gun sites, bunkers etc. Parents were told to warn children not to collect any of these dangerous drugs, especially a worry seeing the German word for Poison was 'GIFT'.

May 28th fishing restrictions were to be removed at last and soon there would be plenty of fish. Once more after years of restrictions fisherman may fish as they please, day or night, as long as they kept within 5 miles of any of the Channel Islands. Certain restrictions were still in force around Alderney and the Casquets but for the rest of the fishing grounds they were now cleared of mines. Petrol also at this time was now available for the boats.

Islanders were still requested to retain and carry their identity cards after Liberation and many were brought to court for being 'cardless'. One man's answer when questioned a Mr John Roberts of the Forest — 'I burnt it because I was fed up seeing the German stamp on it'. '5/- fine' was the answer from the magistrates. Courts were also kept busy as much thieving was still going on.

On *May 28th* an addition to the permanent weekly rations had been decided on for the week-end.
12oz of mince meat loaf and 8oz of ox tongue.
1lb biscuits.
1lb flour, 2ozs baking powder.
3ozs dried fruit.
4ozs either rice, oatmeal or pulses.
Children under 14 years of age would receive a permanent weekly ration of 3ozs of chocolate!

I must have been pleased to have read that! Apparently though, chocolates and sweets did not come fully off ration until early in the 1950s in the Island and also of course, the mainland. Salt must have still been in short supply as I had noted May 18th there were many depots and collection points for sea water still around the Island, selling just like it had been for many many months previously.

PERMITS TO TRAVEL May 23rd

Application for permission to travel to the U.K. on compassionate or other grounds had to be sought through the Guernsey Emigration, then if recommended and considered urgent, to the U.K. authorities. Finally then placed on an 'awaiting passage list'.

With the Island slowly getting back to normality it was not time yet to welcome holiday-makers. Most of the hotels and boarding houses were in a terrible state of repair where the Germans had lived, they also had stolen furniture and removed fittings etc., the repairing and fitting out of the same would take a very long while. Holiday makers were not able to return in sizeable numbers until 1947. The same being for family homes, some being destroyed altogether and many others just unfit to live in for a very long while. The Guernsey families still on the mainland would get priority of course and the majority were very eager to return to their loved ones; but they also had to wait a while. In the meantime some 15 patients were to leave by plane to receive medical treatment on the mainland. (May 28th).

Towards the end of June services to and from the Island came into operation once more. A service by air between Croydon and Guernsey began. Parcel post was resumed to the mainland three times a week (letters were already coming and going). Also the telephone service was re-opened to and from the mainland and Jersey. With the onset of the volume of traffic expected, calls of three minutes duration to the mainland would only be possible and even besides this ruling, long delays were experienced. Understandably, everyone wanted to talk and catch up on five years' separation.

Now at long last June 12th the 8,000 plus radios which had been called in by the Germans could gradually be collected and owners were notified to collect them at 'Victoria Chapel', Victoria Road. Many were beyond repair but approx. 70 per cent of the first 2,000 were in almost the same condition as when handed in, but most people did not get their "wireless' sets back, many had been 'loaned' to the Germans and the majority of the rest had been exported following the June invasion. Other buildings on the Island also held confiscated goods. Cameras also that had been called in were found mainly in a 'mouldy' condition and many had gone missing — most people lost these too, not surprising after being handed around the forces and being stored away for five years. A few islanders still did have their radios, those who had decided not to hand them over (and also the forbidden crystal sets) but for most, amplifiers were placed at many vantage points all over the Town for the locals to listen to the transmission. The world news was broadcast and I remember very well the special recordings made by the Channel Islanders on the mainland. The reception was clear and a large number of Islanders listened to the messages over this new local wave length. Life was certainly so much happier and the streets around St. Peter Port was so much sweeter! Yes I remember very well then the smelly streets; passing some houses where so many P.O.W.s were crowded together smelt very strong — terrible! Also I remember mum and dad did not like us walking up certain streets on our way to school — there were always the soldiers about and 'ladies' that were not nice living there. We could not understand the reason why, but on these occasions did as we were told! How lovely it was to walk anywhere and feel safe and free. Many though were relieved that at last bus services were resumed (June 9th) by the Wayfarer and the Guernsey Railway. Bus fares which were operating during 1940 were increased by 50 per cent. i.e. town to Vazon 9d, town to L'Ancresse 6d and minimum fare 2d!

CHAPTER 5

THE REHABILITATION AND
AT LONG LAST *THE* HOMECOMING!

It was very important too that the Cargo Boat Service was under way bringing more cargo *but* what was more important then, was the thought of 'Islanders' the 'Sarnians' returning home once more. I remember these times very well and the most ('exciting' is the wrong word') memorable for us and for so many was to make a trip down to the 'Weighbridge' to see who had come home. Seeing the Harbour (White Rock) was still mined and dangerous for the general public, lines of people waited at the Weighbridge for the travellers to walk from the boat down the harbour and then between the rows of their loved ones and well wishers. The very first boat load of less than a 100 was a disappointment to many, but there were many touching scenes — tears, hugs and smiles, but no cheering or flags waving. Everyone felt very emotional inside, even we young people, we just sensed the feelings of gratitude.

June 26th 1945 was the first of such reunions, our Liberation Day being May 9th so I'm sure those few weeks between must have seemed like years with many impatient, as within only 48 hours of the Home Office announcement that people could return 7,000 evacuees had applied for permission. Can you imagine such scenes after the hurried evacuation and confusion of 1940 when just no-one knew what to do for the best? The Weighbridge was a 2 minute walk from our home 'Rose Villa' so when the boats were due to arrive — usually three times a week either early morning or early evening time it became a ritual for us to go down. It was wonderful for us youngsters to see the happy and tearful reunions. Also for the older people like my parents and those more elderly who remembered so many of the 'old' faces. It was a continual talking point every time the boat came in. I shall always remember watching out for the boat in the 'roads' from home and then the compelling yet again to see (although weary) the joyous greetings.

On returning, priority was given to women with husbands in Guernsey and Jersey and children of school age. To Channel Islanders who had been deported to Germany but who were now on the mainland staying in hostels, (also living with family or friends) as they had been freed earlier. Also to people wanted for key posts in the re-organisation of island industries and those where work was waiting for them in the building and decorating line, then afterwards came the demobilised servicemen and women and ex-prisoners of war on compassionate leave. The proportion of evacuees from Guernsey was much larger than from Jersey and the proportion returning was two thirds for Guernsey, one third for Jersey. I suppose it was a strange feeling for us youngsters to see the children returning with their name tags pinned on their clothing and mothers frantically looking from one to the other, looking for their own. It so easily could have been us, with mum looking. One can only imagine the feelings of parents and perhaps the bewilderment of the children. We knew when large groups of children and grown-ups too were returning as we could hear them singing on the mail-boat 'Isle of Guernsey' when coming through the pierheads which again included 'Sarnia Cherie', but many others too choked with emotion to sing I'm sure. Five years! what a long time to be separated, being a grand-parent now I would think it tragic not seeing my grandchildren for all those years. They grow and change so quickly, a fortnight's holiday and separation is long enough for André and I.

One reunion I do remember very vividly was meeting with my uncle again (Michael Brassel — my father's half brother). Because nearly all our male relations and of course, my mother, father, sister, myself, uncles and grandparents had stayed in Guernsey together with 23,000 other islanders throughout the whole of the Occupation, it was quite a surprise for me to meet him again. I don't know if I had remembered him then from pre-war days, as I was only eight years old in 1939, but on seeing him, smart in this Royal Air Force uniform, I just cried and cried in his arms. I had been visiting the dear aunt of mine (Mrs. Winnie Salmon) on this particular day and was most surprised to see him walk in. I just couldn't get over the emotion which I felt then. All men in British uniform were looked upon as heroes and their uniform I suppose was unfamiliar to us — being so used to the 'others'. Even though I was aged fourteen, I had realised how they had fought for our freedom and how wonderful life was like now since they had arrived. It was afterwards that hearing of countries and its peoples which had had a terrible time, also camps which had seen so much torture, killings etc., that we all considered ourselves lucky. Despite privations, separations and near starvation, life could have been far worse for us all.

The White Rock was again re-opened August 30th to the public and the boats with passengers continued to arrive — at most with 886 for both Guernsey and Jersey. By mid November all islanders who wished to return would be back. By the end of October 12,000 of the approximately 18,000 who had applied to return would be back on Guernsey soil again. Some 4,000 who had gone away had not applied to come back — some were still in the Forces and naturally many had made their homes after falling in love and were quite comfortable where they were. Like many on the mainland, many Guernsey families were split because of the war. Again, a matter of interest — Boat charges then:

Fares to Southampton first class single £2.10s.0d, and return £4.5s.8d.

Second class £1.13s.2d. and return £2.14s.4d.

First class single to Jersey 11s.11d and return 18s.7d.

Second class 8s.2d. and return 13s.5d!

Did you have to think to work the price out? I did!

I have spoken recently to a friend who because she paid for her fare back home travelled on the ship 'Hantonia' during late May or early June, before the main evacuees began to return. With her husband still abroad in the 'Air Force' she returned with her 2 year old baby son, but was appalled at the lack of food and commodities on the Island. Although rationed too on the mainland there was a vast difference here and although the islanders who stayed thought they were in the land of plenty — it was not so and she was worried and quite concerned for the well-being of her son. Apparently the doctors' surgeries were being kept busy too with the children returning. With our tomatoes being so plentiful, the children's bodies (unlike ours) just could not accept all the acid intake and they came out in a rash all over their bodies. She, like many others had let her little one fill up on tomatoes!

She remarked too that *no* alcohol was available at all and feelings at that time so soon after Liberation were running very high amongst 'some' who stayed, against those very few who had fraternized and collaborated with the Germans, and which was felt could maybe lead to trouble after having a drink or two. Though I'm sure a good cup of tea with other 'goodies' coming in was much more appreciated by everyone!

With families returning again and setting up homes, furniture was scarce and expensive to buy — Mr. Bougourd writes — November 8th many refugees roaming about now looking for houses and their furniture. Some are lucky to find a good deal, others not so lucky. Most are glad to be back again. Almost 1,000 islanders are homeless but are being helped and billeted at 'Hotel de France Hostel', St. Peter Port. The Island is slowly settling down.

As regards to André and his family returning — his brother John like many other islanders was still abroad in the Army (in the Greek Islands) his sister Therese had met a Wolverhampton boy, married and had naturally wanted to stay — so it was only André with his mum and dad returning. They had originally left their home at 5 Contree Mansell and on returning found no-one living there and the rooms completely bare of furniture. Their old friends and neighbours from before the evacuation immediately got in touch with them and told them where all their furniture and belongings were. They had been used and taken by a local family, but to be fair — after seeing this family most of the furniture was returned the next day with no arguments. The blame could not always be on the 'others' — the Enemy. Because of instances like this feelings between islanders sometimes were not at all pleasant at first — I'm sure some islanders must have wondered if perhaps they had done the right thing in returning — would they have been better off staying? in work? in surroundings they had got used to? with their new made friends? and now returning to perhaps nothing except resentment like André came up against when trying to make new friends. Perhaps these one or two were in a minority but like characters everywhere, some can be so unkind. With André arriving back with many hundreds of others — a new life with new friends had to begin again, I expect difficult at the age of $17^{1}/_{2}$. He joined the St. Peter Port Boys' Club and it was not long before he came up against some nasty remarks with very strong language, 'you left us and was a yellow bellied ... etc ... etc' (Remembering the 'don't be yellow — STAY' posters at the harbour in 1940) André felt he had put up with enough bullying with being thought of as a 'froggie' whilst at Woverhampton (see later) — not a happy time, and he really couldn't understand the strong feelings of these two particular young chaps. Enough was enough and one day André spoke out and reminded him that it hadn't been easy for his family coming home to find little of their furniture. André also at the time felt priority was given to those who stayed when applying for jobs and he had no choice whatsoever, and on the mainland life had been hard for his family with many shortages too and raids to contend with, mentioning life here was more safe than the continentals had who were also under the Nazis — finishing up with 'if' we had all stayed, more of you would have starved ... etc ... etc. Heated words between the two and an invitation from André to meet with bare fists apparently did not come to anything. They did not (pleased to say) finish up in the St. Peter Port Boxing Ring at the club! But I do think this highlights some of the feelings at the time. I just remember and know mum and dad were very happy to see everyone home again and the vast majority were thrilled to be back, but the rehabilitation period was not plain sailing for many.

48

The authorities stored and collected a great deal of furniture and allowed families to see if they could find the furniture they had left behind — not an easy task for anyone, nor for the authorities in charge plus some resentment and grievances amongst a few. It must have been for some, a difficult time. A time for adjustment in some cases even had to be made within families too. I know and had heard of brothers and sisters, some had stayed, some went away (especially with those young people coming up to teenage years and a little older) who had to learn to live together once more with different ideas and a totally different outlook on life after so long apart. Not easy and much patience was needed. I'm sure the Germans split up many a family home through the long separation.

Since our Liberation, many vacancies were advertised in the situations vacant columns in our newspapers, mostly, work was available in the growing line and in vineries, where André started work.

On farms too, much work in hand for the islanders to restore and build up the once famous cattle breeds in both islands. Many had been slaughtered by the Germans. We children were indeed lucky to have such quality of milk throughout and although rationed, we enjoyed what was given. Unfortunately so did the Germans and they stole many cows. German prisoners were photographed returning some before having to leave the island and before going on to 'landing crafts' which had been used for our Liberation to bring our troops and goods to us. (Daily Sketch, May 16th.)

Growers now had a new lease of life and as early as July our famous tomatoes were being exported again to the mainland; also beans and cucumbers. Much work continued to get the restrictions of imports and Guernsey produce relaxed, therefore allowing growers to send their produce to any buyer in any area on the mainland. November 6th was the date the restrictions were at last relaxed. Although everyone had Ration Books and were in line with the mainland rations, the town was busy again. At long last shops were beginning to fill with goods once more — those empty and boarded up re-opened and the 'dummy' packages replaced in other shop windows.

Woolworths were advertising for 'old staff' from before the war to apply for work and when re-opened selling goods more than 6d. (maximum) like it had been before the war started, no-one minded paying the extra! Guernsey was thoroughly spoilt from 1945 for a year or two as the Government treated us as 'export' and the shops were selling only the best.

August 26th saw potatoes off ration for the first time in a very long while and petrol would soon be off ration. The first new vehicles for businesses had arrived on July 27th and six tractors for agriculture on

August 1st. Our annual famous 'Battle of Flowers' resumed again during August 1945 also the Sark Cattle Show. Everything in quite a short while was getting sorted out and into place once more. It was with great gratitude that Guernsey had been 'spring cleaned' so to speak and it really was rather a sad time to see a large consignment of Liberation Troops leave on September 3rd. A great crowd were gathered to see them leave the harbour and Angela Falla (a well known and popular soloist) sang (what else) yes — 'Sarnia Cherie'. A touching tribute to these heroes of ours who faced a mammoth task to clear the Islands of five years accumulation of arms etc. The men of the main Force 135 left on 25th September, but pleased to say some of these gents still visit Guernsey for our Liberation Day celebrations even now. A special annual programme is laid on for these welcome guests for their week's enjoyment during early May.

FISH & CHIPS AND CUSTARD TARTS!

October 8th, 1945 saw the opening once again of the 'Gaumont Palace' in St Julian's Avenue. It was also found to be in a very sorry state and needed a complete overhaul after an 18 month closure. This was to be another special event for us islanders to see the opening with three performances daily, with a change of weekly programmes too! 'Pardon my Sarong' was the first feature film shown with the famous comedians, Lou Abott and Bud Costello. We had three cinemas at this time as the 'North Cinema' at St Sampson's was also in full swing.

October 4th was the day when a regular boat service to Sark began. 'The Celia' was licensed to carry 12 passengers.

Yes a large heading on 'The Star' newspaper — October 13th — Fish & Chips on sale next week, fat had at last been released! Cakes and confectionary to follow soon! November 3rd another large heading on the front page of our local newspaper CUSTARD TARTS AGAIN! Also deliveries of bread to be resumed soon. Hopefully too our famous Guernsey Gâche would soon be in the shops again. Up to November 3rd — no allocation of dried fruits or dried eggs had been issued, so the likes of fruit cakes, madeiras, sponge cakes, swiss rolls and Guernsey Gâche were out of the question but custard tarts and vanilla slices should be available within a week. (I've wondered if they were my favourite then, like they are today).

December 14th, 1945 another great and joyous day and this time it was Alderney's turn. This was the day when the first party of 88 'ordinary' family people were allowed back home.

An original Christmas greeting card I found amongst mum's photographs

December 27th, bright new Guernsey pennies and half pennies were now in circulation bearing the year '1945'. Totalling £850, they were the first local coins to be minted since 1938. At long last these saw the final use and disappearance of the ugly and drab pfennigs. I'm sure the gas meters were most happy to accept the new coins and like us all, were also able to thrive well on the new diet!

What an eventful year it had been one can hardly believe what changes had taken place within the 12 months of 1945 — from near starvation in December 1944 to having so much in December 1945 — I'm sure folk must have wondered if it was really all happening. . . .

As you can imagine, we children then were being spoiled with special film shows, and a *Party* for everyone! Apparently we children were asked to take half of our milk ration so that the other half could be made into butter to allow a tea party to be served worthy of the occasion. Aren't we and all children lucky now? Most times everything is just taken for granted and really my young grandchildren seem to be invited to parties every other week. A friend of mine, Mrs. Browning of the German Underground Hospital told me once after reading my book — she knew why I had written that I could not remember any of my birthdays or Christmases as a child during the Occupation — simply because those times were no different from any other days, every day was the same with no special treats.

Well, we did have treats afterwards and I'm positive by the reading of Mr. William Bourgourd's (Bill's) Diary (a great character and friend) that his treats were every mealtime of every day just being with his loving family once more. His wife and two young sons were evacuated to Baildon in Yorkshire and he explains how he felt missing them so much and then seeing them once again and after so long a separation. His younger son Roy was only three when leaving in 1940 so naturally he would not remember his Dad, Billy was aged five but it took much love, patience and time to all become pals. Probably writing helped Mr. Bougourd — his day-to-day diary helped keep him going even though if caught by the Germans it would have been a serious offence. I was amazed to see the volumes he had written. Thousands of foolscap pages of his life and interests since the age of four years. I have been grateful to him for allowing me to read his account especially of the rehabilitation period and for dates which I never would have remembered. It helps greatly to have a reminder of those good times and I sincerely hope at his age of 86 I shall have the same wonderful memory like Mr. Bougourd still has — a remarkable man. Also my sincere thanks to a good friend Alf Le Poidevin who loaned me local newspapers of the rehabilitation period. He also has vivid memories of the Occupation and of the frights he had.

The following year May 9th 1946 was again one of those special days we all remember as it was the first of many Liberation Day Cavalcade and Celebrations to remember and give thanks. After Thanksgiving services all over the Island, a large cavalcade of children, grown ups colourfully dressed either walking or on bicycles, with horse drawn vehicles or by other means and decorated passed in procession along the sea front. Also a Military Band and a fly past by an Air Force display team. Thousands of Islanders turned out — all had a wonderful day and the evening ended with a glorious firework display. Today many older islanders like Alf much prefer to remember our Special Day quietly at home and give thanks with his wife who had stayed with him throughout the Occupation.

With firms now wanting to renew business with the Channel Islands and with new advertising material having appeared now in our local newspapers such as 'wise people — take a good tonic and keep fit and cheerful' and 'Woman of 75 could sing for joy!'. For better health and looks take Juno-Junipah!' Everything in the garden looked rosy and there were many other happy days to follow May 9th 1945.

8th June, 1946

TO-DAY, AS WE CELEBRATE VICTORY, I send this personal message to you and all other boys and girls at school. For you have shared in the hardships and dangers of a total war and you have shared no less in the triumph of the Allied Nations.

I know you will always feel proud to belong to a country which was capable of such supreme effort; proud, too, of parents and elder brothers and sisters who by their courage, endurance and enterprise brought victory. May these qualities be yours as you grow up and join in the common effort to establish among the nations of the world unity and peace.

George R.I.

CHAPTER 6

ANOTHER SCHOOL MOVE AND
WORK BEGINS

Now the children had or were returning from many parts of the mainland; mostly they had been billeted or had lived in Scotland, the South West and the northern towns and cities where it was reasonably safe from air raids. Initially the States Intermediate School was situated in Rosaire Avenue, but the school had been taken over and commandeered so I was taught with others at Burnt Lane School.

We schoolchildren were given time off school until 14th May but were joined at the end of September at Rosaire Avenue – once more when the school was made habitable for our use again. The girls who had attended the Intermediate School before the war had now returned with their teachers from Rochdale, where they had lived and attended school during the war years. Many have since said how very happy they were there and the many 'aunties and uncles' were thought a lot of. Quite a close bond developed between them, understandably being together for five years. I am sure the same affection was felt between scholars and school teachers too, as they in turn and in most cases, took the role as mothers and fathers. We who stayed, had also our close friends, and for a while, there was a division at school, us and them, but we all soon settled in and mixed well, getting to know new friends and new teachers. With reference to our school work, although not as advanced as a thirteen year old of today, we were more or less on a par with each other, the Rochdale and the Occupation girls.

I left school the following March at fourteen years old and began office work at the States Telephone Department. My wage then was 15/- a week. I gave my Mother 10/- and I was allowed to keep 5/- for myself for clothing and a visit to the cinema in the 1/3d.s! Thursday evenings was the family weekly picture night and seats were regularly booked at the Regal Cinema in Upland Road. We would get there early usually to listen to Kennedy Bott and the wonderful organ. Mum and Dad had regular complimentary seats in the back row at the

'Gaumont', St. Julians Avenue, for many years on Saturday evenings. Sadly both cinemas have now been demolished, one for offices and the other for a large car park.

We teenagers knew nothing of fashion during the Occupation years and this trend continued afterwards. Looking back on photographs, we dressed very ordinarily in plain practical clothes. We and our parents just did not have much money to spend and if I remember rightly, clothes were rationed for quite a while after the war ended.

My late teens brought in the new look, very long skirts and I was the proud owner of one! A donkey brown one — I remember it well. I was a member of the Ebenezer Church choir and social evenings and outings with the club were much enjoyed by everyone. My main interest was being attached to the Church, I was also a member of the then Girls' Life Brigade and continued helping to become a Cadet Leader and a Sunday School teacher. The young children seemed to find Miss Finigan a mouthful, so I was known and called Miss Vinegar by my class! Strangely enough one of these boys (now a man of course) still says the same, I'm sure! Mind you, better perhaps than Mrs. Bidet! or Mrs. B. O. like visitors and children have called me in the past! BIHET is pronounced B-A in French, the sounding of the H is dropped.

I always had a soft spot for the very poor children from the larger families in my little class. Most Sundays after school we would visit a very dear old lady living in the Canichers, Miss Lily Sauvarin who was terribly crippled and could not help herself in any way, not even with her own feeding. Her one pleasure as she laid in bed close by the window was to smile to everyone as they passed and waved. She was always ready to smile and had a great Christian faith. She just loved watching and listening to the five or six year olds singing their little choruses; and I was always amazed then how she and her elderly friend Miss Gympton (who was stone deaf) and who looked after her every need, kept so contented. I could never forget these two rather special people.

Working at the States Telephone Department, I was very lucky to work for ten years with Irene and with such happy and sincere friends, both men and women. We all got on well and it was a pleasure working together. We sometimes worked long hours — 8.45 a.m. to 7.45 p.m., with three hours overtime especially a necessity when the quarterly accounts had to be sent out. All of us couples got on very well and of course are still friends today.

Everyday, four times a day, my work took me up and down St. Julian's Avenue, a wonderful tree-lined avenue, which now is still struggling to look something like it used to. Sadly it was in 1948 the Elm trees were considered dangerous and had to be cut down, mostly they were found to be hollow.

St Julians Avenue prior to 1948

Mum and dad's friends of many years, our aunt Edie and uncle Bill Wilcox, had owned and incidentally built Perry Nook Tea Rooms (now the West Coast Restaurant), with dad's help and guidance. If I could, with my mother, I used to help them at weekends, but my favourite weekends were spent at Vazon with Irene and where Peggy (Bodkin) and family used to meet — it seems to me now it used to be almost every weekend, and always knowing they'd be there in the same spot on Vazon beach.

Isn't it strange that when one is younger, the sun always seemed to be shining and everyone seemingly always happy. They were great times, and with a lovely family, I was sure too of a bonus with a good mixed picnic! I was called the 'dustbin' (nothing's changed!) as I always seemed to finish up all their goodies. Perhaps I was just making up for the five lost years, eh?

Great friends of mum and dad.
Edie and Billy Wilcox.

CHAPTER 7

THE BATTLING 'BIHETS' AND 'MON REVE' — MY DREAM!

André's grandparents were born in Normandy and because their parents were opposed to the wedding, they fled and eloped to Jersey and married there. André's father, Marcel George, and his brothers and sisters, were all born in Jersey. André's mother, Marie Josephine, was born in Brittany, then as a baby was brought over by her mother, Madame Allain and settled in Guernsey. André's father and family moved from Jersey to Alderney, then eventually settled in Guernsey where he met Marie Josephine, a typical little French lady — hence the arrival of the Bihet family and André Pierre Joseph!

There had been an article written in the Jersey Evening Post and in a French newspaper during the 1914–1918 War reporting on the 'Battling Bihets at War'. Apparently the five brothers were all fighting at the front, and all survived the First World War. André's uncle (his mother's brother) won the Croix de Guerre and Le Militaire Medal — high awards for his bravery, but was sadly killed.

André (my patient and long suffering husband since 'A Child's War' and now having 'Reflections' to contend with) was also born in St. Peter Port at 'Woodlands Cottage' in the Bouet. It has been demolished since and the very busy 'B & Q' Store stands in its place, the car park was once their large garden. He was the youngest in a family of seven children, all born in Guernsey, but of different fathers. His father was Marcel George Bihet and worked as a stoker at the Guernsey Gas Company. His mother was tragically widowed three times and had a hard struggle to bring up her children — having to work at several different jobs to feed and clothe the family. André was really brought up during his early years by his French grandmother who could not speak a word of English. All the children had a special job to do, helping in the house and the garden and then selling fruit and vegetables around at the neighbours, the children pushing a cart around with the goods.

The family also kept a smallholding, keeping and killing the livestock. 'Rosie' the pet dog let all and sundry come through the garden gate but apparently would not let anyone out, especially if they were scrumping apples and sometimes being caught up the tree! I suppose the interest of growing in those days has always stayed with André (except when he left school in Wolverhampton and worked on machinery for small parts of war planes) and when he returned to Guernsey, began work at the Caledonia Nursery. For 44 years he worked there and for the best part of his life found the work interesting. His work included propagating shrubs with floristry work and with much interest growing oranges, lemons, tangerines etc. Wreath making and bouquets were made by André and Roy Le Poidevin, his working mate for all that length of time. They also decorated different hotels and venues for V.I.P.s and Royalty on special visits. André had the honour of making bouquets and posies for Her Majesty and other royal V.I.P.s during this time.

André was 12 years old and at school at St. Joseph's (Catholic School) in 1940. He remembers meeting very early in the morning (before 6 a.m.) at the school with a small carrier bag containing a little lunch, a change of under clothing and a few coppers. I expect, that was about it. Children were to be evacuated together as a school with some teachers willing to go and travel with them. Some 1,000 children (and babies and toddlers) like myself stayed but many more, almost 5,000 either travelled with the school or with their parents (mostly with mothers) on to the boats. No-one knew what to do for the best and there was confusion at home and at the schools and harbours. Noticeboards were contradicting, some saying 'Go' others 'Don't be yellow stay at home!' What a terrible time for families making such decisions. André eventually left with some of his schoolfriends and after a long weary journey arrived in Weymouth where the children were looked after and given food etc. They all eventually arrived in Scotland. He remembers very well being lined up at 'Dixon Hall' with the others and being looked over by prospective 'foster parents' — not very pleasant for them I'm sure but maybe there were some boys of André's age who were thinking more of it all as an adventure. Anyway, André did not enjoy this inspection and was not chosen so was taken with other boys from the school and looked after in a Catholic Church Hall on Paisley Road where he waited for news — hoping his parents, brothers and sisters would be able to trace where he was. He had no idea where they might be, nor had the other children — still at home in Guernsey or on the mainland. After about four months probably due to a formed 'Channel Island Society' they eventually found each other and settled in a small terraced home in Wolverhampton.

60

It was at the Church Hall that one day he was most surprised and couldn't believe if he was seeing right as the gentleman talking to his teacher Mr Cooper looked very much like his dad! He looked again and sure enough it was. André remembers this day very well and it didn't take him long to get ready to join him and meet up with his mother again too.

Whilst André and his family lived in Wolverhampton for the five years, life was most unhappy for André at school. He was slightly built, rather quiet and shy and his name 'André Bihet' made him a target for bullies. He also had spoken much more French at home than English so to the older boys he was definitely a 'Froggie'. Everyday there were incidents and children can be very cruel as everyone knows. André could not take his tales home either as his mother (although a good mother), would have given him another bashing! It must have been a very trying time also for his parents as there were four separate families living in the terraced cottage, making 11 people in all. For Islanders to live away from the sea too must have been miserable for a time. This is the one thing most Islanders miss when away from the Island. I can well remember going on our first holiday with the family touring Devon and Cornwall and every corner we turned just expected to and hoped the sea would be there. Just a glance of it! A lot of Guernsey people evacuated to cities and towns must have taken many months getting used to their new surroundings.

On arriving back and coming in to the entrance of our harbour at St. Peter Port must have been a most wonderful sight, there is no harbour more picturesque, especially first thing in the morning with the sun shining on the sea and hillside.

On returning André and his family were again 'Townies' and you would have thought at some time he and I would have met in such a small island. But no — he first saw me on Waterloo Station! Being a member and with my interest with the Ebenezer Church I was asked whether I would like to join other young people and travel to Wimbledon and to Southlands College for a 'Methodist Christian Conference'. This I did and with a thousand others thoroughly enjoyed the friends, fellowship and learning too, as at that time I did think I would like to become a missionary. Well it was whilst saying and kissing farewell to friends from the West Country at the station that I apparently caught André's eye — he tells everyone that I was making a meal of it(!) and wondered who I was. André was with friends from Guernsey who had spent a weekend in London (André had won a little on the pools!) and was like us on the way home. As it happened my cousin Les Collins was with him and told him who I was.

Well it seems to me, I changed a lot at this time (I was 18) and after this began to go out more and got to enjoy meeting and dancing (!)

with other young people. My thoughts of becoming a missionary were forgotten.

On Saturdays, our age group, late teens and early twenties, would meet at St. George's Hall on the Esplanade for dancing. Listening to the sound of the Georgians was a real treat, so much rhythm and good timing and we had so much space to 'quickstep'. It had a wonderful large floor and at special dances, Victory Balls and the like, easily 1,000 people could be dancing with room to spare. Although basic, and the seats (like cinema seats in rows) were tatty, there was a grand atmosphere. It was only on special licence (perhaps a New Year's Eve Ball) that alcohol was allowed to be served, so despite no drink, everyone was happy and enjoyed themselves. During the week, roller skating was held, again enjoyed by many, but not me. I did not have the courage to try it. But it was here at St. George's Hall that André asked me to dance and where we whirled round and round the large ballroom with the quick step!

I met André during the month of December, we courted for two years, got engaged in the December and two years later, again in December, we married at St. Joseph's Catholic Church on December 9th, 1954. It seemed to be the normal time to get to know one another and to save to get a home and furniture together. Four years does seem a long time now but one had to save out of low wages to get the basics, no borrowing or credit cards for us, nor for most.

With André working as a gardener, or more precisely as a Nurseryman (propagating etc.) at the Caledonia Nursery, Fosse André, he managed to work much overtime during the light evenings to help keep his widowed mother and to save a little each week towards our future home. He was very proud to have bought our main furniture, cash paid £354, which consisted of a settee suite, dining room suite, bedroom suite, a carpet square *and* a glass cabinet. No washing machines for us then, nor fridges or carpet sweepers — gas boilers, outside wall cupboard and dustpan and brush!

Our first home was a cottage 'Mon Reve' (My Dream) at La Ramée and we lived there for seven years. Whilst living there, our two daughters, Sally and Carole were born — Sally on December 15th, 1955 and Carole on December 21st, 1959. All of our important dates seemed to be in December and all unplanned!

They were happy days — happy Island. Guernsey was peaceful, quiet and friendly. Everyone knew each other and chatted. Yes, we all had time for each other then. There was Phyl our milk lady who came every day and had a cuppa and with mum also; Policemen popping in for coffee; bread roundsmen; the delivery of vegetables, meat and groceries, they were all good friends.

With fewer cars, people walked everywhere, met and always had time to natter. I remember so well the cries of 'Mackerel' and 'Fisho', selling from vans along the street, beautiful fresh fish and crabs, a shilling each, or three mackerel for a bob!

The bus drivers also used to drop us at our front doors and picked us up on route anywhere. The roads were quiet, so very different from today's traffic.

CHAPTER 8

A MOVE TO 'ROSEDALE' & GUESTS

One day out of the blue, my father — whom you may remember as being Bill Finigan and having a small building business, visited us at Mon Reve on his usual daily morning pop-in for a coffee and a chat. He surprised me by saying he had just come away from a house auction right opposite Beau Sejour and had bought the property for £2,400 (in 1962.) He wanted André and I to see it and if we liked what we saw, we could move in! Although the cottage was now rather small and cramped with our two daughters, we really had not thought of moving for a while but felt Dad's offer was good and he seemed keen for us to see the house for ourselves.

André and I went to see 'Rosedale' the next day with my father. Oh dear, it was large, cold looking and brown walls everywhere, even doors and large shutters! Everywhere needed a lot of work and just where to start? Eight large high ceilinged rooms, all neglected and so dark. I secretly shed a few tears which set me thinking I just did not want to leave the cosy cottage we had enjoyed for seven years. My father could imagine the end results of hard work as he was in the business, but told us we need not worry or decide to move, it was entirely up to us. He just wanted us to be happy and being dad, that was him, always wanting to do the right thing for us.

We could not have had a more wonderful father. André always thought of him then as his best friend and even now when talking of him, will always say the same.

So really as much to please him as anyone, and with encouragement from the girls — they loved the large conservatory and sunny garden at the back — we decided to move and set to work.

Once we had started, we grew to love the house. Every room was different. The top rooms had a sloping ceiling with fitted window seats — so attractive and with a lovely outlook across the park.

It was during an evening with Dad and André painting that my father suggested we could start a guesthouse. Me. I thought, taking guests? Oh no, I would be too nervous and I did have young children to consider. Sally was six and Carole two years old, I was still very busy with them. But I gave the matter some thought and decided to give it a try as I had been working at different hotels waiting on tables and at different banquets and functions. André babysat and I earned a little doing this during the evenings. Dad said I was a good cook and that I knew what people wanted on the table. This was true as you learn quite a lot working and walking through hotel kitchens!

We decided to start with just two couples in two large airy rooms which the States Tourist Committee were very happy to register. That's how we started and continued taking guests for twenty-seven years.

Our first four guests in 1962 were very friendly and we all got on so well that they helped to perhaps ease the little nervous feelings I felt cooking during that first week. André finished work at five and always helped with the dishing up and washing up every evening, no rest but what an interesting and happy life we shared. We have met people from so many walks of life and really have not had too much trouble at all. We respected everyone that came and treated them as we would want to be treated should we be on holiday. With this treatment, we always received the same respect back and it really was a pleasure meeting new and old friends back year after year.

I think it is a shame that there are so few small family guest houses left in Guernsey. People liked the personal attention, plenty of good food, the clean home and the welcoming cup of tea always worked wonders!

Going back to our first guests from Worcester, Kath, Fred, John and Margaret, they were all ready to enjoy themselves and have a laugh which was just as well as when I knocked and opened the bedroom door taking their morning cup of tea, facing me was Kath and Fred lying very lop-sided. One side of the bed had collapsed on the floor during the night, trapping Kath more or less on the floor with Fred, not able to avoid resting and laying on her. What a surprise and shock! It was our bed and we had never had any mishaps before. In those days beds had springs, no 'boxes' for mattresses to sit on like the modern divans of today. Most guesthouse owners moved out with their children to lesser bedrooms (ours was on the top floor) during the season and we had done just that, never expecting our double bed to collapse on the first night too!

Anyway our guests took it all in good part and were literally doubled up with laughter when I walked in. Thankfully, they were not hurt and the bolts were renewed the same day.

When we first started taking guests in 1962, we always cooked a traditional roast beef lunch and a rice pudding for afterwards on Sundays. When guests made a return visit, I tried to make a change

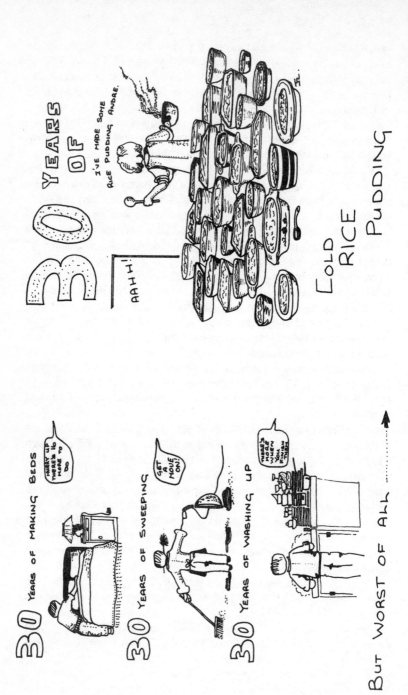

sometimes from rice pudding but they always wanted to know why, (friend John thinks otherwise)! A fresh crab salad was also offered for tea, so it meant all morning was spent cooking and the afternoon we were picking the crab. As always, we did ask these four guests if they would like crab. Well they said they would try it but weren't too sure. Anyway, we picked the crab meat as usual but had obtained four extra lady crabs (as we call them), so before they sat down, we placed a cooked crab still in their shells at each of their places. We waited and watched their reaction from the crack of the kitchen door. Well, we had never seen such expressions — we could read what they were thinking — "How on earth are we going to tackle these". Much fun and lovely to remember as it has only been this Christmas that we heard of Kath's death last year and Fred a couple of years ago. There are many we still keep in touch with and we know that friends like Kath and Fred will never be forgotten.

During these early catering days, we also had to keep an eye on Carole, she wandered into the dining room one evening and came across a little package under Bob's chair. It was only his false teeth which she paraded around with and showed everyone! Poor Bob had tried to quietly remove his teeth when he ate but he had not bargained for Carole being so inquisitive. As it happened he felt nothing against Carole and everyone had a good laugh. Bob, Anne (his wife), Edna and Andy their friends all came together and loved taking Sally and Carole on trips with them, either to Grande Rocques which was their favourite beach and several times to Herm for the day. They were all good friends and lovely people. Edna and Andy telephoned me after learning of mum's death in 1991 and both were crying quite unashamedly on the telephone to me. Passing on good and sad news about the family are always an interest to them. Unfortunately we don't see them now but still keep in touch with these dear old friends from way back. (Sadly now, 1993, Andy is no longer with us).

After a couple of years went by, my father suggested that he put a corrugated roof on part of the large conservatory at the back of the house to make two "summer" bedrooms for us and the girls. As the floor was concrete and we were very private at the back, it made sense as I was now very confident and happy catering for four adults and sometimes with children. Mind you, there was a question put to Carole at school about home and the answer was 'Mummy, daddy, Sally and me sleep in the greenhouse' amongst other answers!

Apart from heavy rain disturbing us on the corrugated roof at night, we slept well and we could now cater for eight adults comfortably. Before a permit was granted, the Fire Chief made us install a 'Davy Line' which had to be tried and tested, also by me from the second floor. Oh dear, it did seem a very high building!

Taking in extra guests meant it was not all laughter and fun. There were accidents and sickness of course. Broken legs and arms, children with terrible sunburn and having to get up during the night to take them to the Ambulance Station and one lady who had a miscarriage in the bedroom!

Minor and emergency operations were to take place and a French lady, again a regular visitor was rushed to hospital after suffering some kind of fit at the breakfast table. It was unfortunate too that her English was very limited but at the hospital they sorted out her problems. She came from Quimper and has invited André and I over many times to stay in her 'second' home — a cottage but I don't know why we have never spent a holiday in France. Too close, I expect, but maybe one day!

Back to these ailments! Another poor gentleman who had previously suffered with back problems spent his week's holiday lying flat out on the bedroom floor; and I should add, it was nothing to do with the bed this time!

Other guests had to return to the mainland for loved ones being ill and sometimes for funerals. One family who had to return just had no money left and we offered to lend them some — though in the back of our minds we did not expect to receive it back. Within a fortnight to our surprise back the money came. We were very lucky indeed with all our dealings with guests except for one instance whilst at Woodcote where I had to act quickly. I am sure it was because we were involved with them all and their holidays throughout — we were never in the background so to speak, always at hand to help and answer their questions — really to enjoy their company too, even though most days and evenings it meant a lot of hard work.

MRS. DODD'S REWARD & SURPRISE!

We were still at Rosedale when we had a great coincidence which André and I will never forget. A Mr. and Mrs. Dodd from Wolverhampton booked a holiday and duly arrived. A couple in their sixties whom again we got into conversation easily. In chatting to Mrs. Dodd she told me the main reason for their visit to Guernsey was to try and find out what happened to a 'French' refugee boy who had worked in her workshop where she was the supervisor at the Midland Metal Spinning Company from 1942 to 1945. He had become quite ill and had left work before the war ended. I picked up the 'Midland Metal Spinning Company' as André had worked there and I remembered him saying he had been very ill with jaundice! André as always was washing up dishes, but when I called and he got speaking to Mrs. Dodd they easily realised he was the boy she wanted! There was great excitement and many tears by Mrs. Dodd who had worried so much about this little refugee who was pale and thin and who just never was able to return to work. With families returning to the Island, Mrs. Dodd lost contact. But what a lovely coincidence especially for Mrs. Dodd, she couldn't quite believe her luck and said at the time she was far happier than if she'd been given £5,000.

After this 'special' meeting and very happy holiday, they both returned the following year but very sadly Mr. Dodd suffered a heart attack at our home — he returned after his stay in hospital but unfortunately for them no more holidays in Guernsey.

Another coincidence came to light regarding André's family fairly recently. One day I was signing my books at a table at 'Oatlands Craft Centre' — seeing me writing a lady nearby got talking and said she came from Wolverhampton. She said she had made friends with a Guernsey refugee (again with a French Christian name and surname) and that she had lived next door to her and her family in Melbourne Street. Yes, you've guessed who the teenager was, Andre's sister Marie Therese along with the Bihet family!

Small world, isn't it?

CHAPTER 9

GRAMP AND THE 'OLD' CHARACTERS

'Rose Villa' was very much a family home and had been in my mother's family for well over 100 years. My Great grandfather James Gobear Collins was born May 5th, 1833 and was a lawyer in Guernsey. My grandfather William Joseph also known as 'Joe', 'Pop' or 'Gramp' was born April 12th 1867 at Les Canichers, as was my mother Gladys Elsie on October 19th, 1904, and my sister and I in 1931 and 1933. Of course my mother's brothers and sisters were also born at the house, so you can well understand why my grandfather (Gramp) blessed the invaders in 1940 and why he just was not going to move, nothing would have made him leave his home with all his family memories.

My mother, father, sister and myself had been living in St. John's Street in a tiny three roomed cottage when my grandmother died in 1938. Seeing these papers I thought maybe you would be interested to know the cost of my gran's funeral then and the charges for inscribing the headstone. A similar charge now is more like £1,500. (Pages 72 and 73).

The family then moved down to Rose Villa for my mother to look after old Gramp. I explained how he was a special character in 'A Child's War' and what he did not do and what he should have done during the Occupation. He was a real old 'Guernsey' character and well liked by everyone. We do seem to miss the old characters of the town these days, a few years ago we seemed to have many, just a few I'll mention. There was 'Can-Can' — an elderly bearded gentleman who at one time was a knife and scissor grinder who wore a beret and sometimes a top hat, and who always dressed very peculiarly. He always carried a strange looking nobbly silver decorated walking stick. Apparently during the Occupation he was sent to an internment camp together with Gertie his wife but was often seen before, and in later years riding his bicycle down Bordage and Fountain Street towing his wife behind him. He made a seat for her cut out of a large beer barrel and she sat contentedly whilst he peddled! If not in the barrel (seeing she was very tiny, only 4'4" in height) he would place her in a box cart

My mother as a girl with her mother and father.
Gran and grandpa Collins 1908

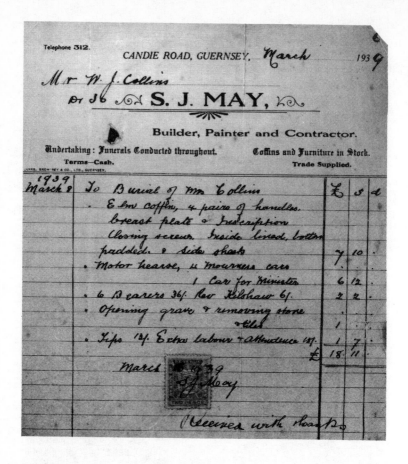

Telephone 312.

CANDIE ROAD, GUERNSEY, *March* 193**9**

M r W. J. Collins

Dr to S. J. MAY,

Builder, Painter and Contractor.

Undertaking: Funerals Conducted throughout.   Coffins and Furniture in Stock.
Terms—Cash.   Trade Supplied.

1939 March 8	To Burial of Mrs Collins	£	s	d
	Elm coffin, 4 pairs of handles. breast plate & inscription Closing screws. Inside lined, bottom padded. & side sheets	7	10	.
	Motor hearse, 4 mourners cars 1 Car for Minister	6	12	.
	6 Bearers 36/. Rev Kilshaw 6/.	2	2	.
	Opening grave & removing stone & tiles	1		.
	Fees 14/. Extra labour + attendence 13/.	1	7	.
	£	18	11	.

March 9 1939
S. J. May

Received with thanks

and tow! Although peculiar in dress and character Can-Can was an intelligent and learned gent, to children though, *very* odd. Then there was a very large well known gentleman, Charlie Duncombe. Being dark in colour and because there was only one such large family, he seemed to always be around the town and to stand out from everyone else. Another large gent who also seemed enormous was Jack Ward, a military style man who always wore hundreds of war medals on his coat. He was a religious man and would preach the gospel around the town; or sing hymns. Before 'Good Friday' he would normally walk around with a crown of 'thorns' on his head with streaks of red running down his face. When quite young I can remember seeing him like this.

There was 'Shaky Bill' another elderly gent whom the boys used to tease around the Canichers area (he lived in the 'Back Canichers') — he was harmless too but would always shake his walking stick at the

72

Mr. J. Collins Canichers

IN ACCOUNT WITH

F. W. OPIE,

Monumental Mason in Marble, Stone and Granite,

ST. JULIAN'S AVENUE, GUERNSEY.

Tel. 668.   Estimates Given.   Charges Moderate.

	£	s	d
Cleaning Headstone		12	6
Painting 5 Coats of White Lead		15	0
Cutting & Blacking 110 Letters			
at 3/- doz letters		1	7	6
Reblacking & Gilding 226 letters			
at 1/3 doz letters		1	8	9
Cartage both ways			8	0
Fixing Tiles and Gravel		10	0
	£	5 - 1 - 9		

Paid with thanks

July 28th 1939

F. W. Opie

boys (and girls!) and chase everyone off, always looking rather
frightening. There was Steve Picquet who lived at Pleinmont in a
converted German Bunker and called it 'On-me-Own' — with only
goats! and he did know all their names! Amos De La Mare was another
one you'd find in the Canichers singing, and marching up Les Cotils to

the hymn 'Onward Christian Soldiers'. You'd find him preaching usually outside Boots both in English and French!

Outside 'The Old Gate House' in the Pollet usually on a Saturday was another gent who entertained with a piccolo.

An enormous man from Guernsey was 'The Glaxo Baby' as everyone knew him, but others also nicknamed him 'BO-PEEP' and he was a window cleaner. He always joined in celebration parades dressed as a baby in blue and white and wearing baby's nappy complete with dummy and pulling a small toy lamb on wheels behind him.

Two ladies come to mind — one known as the 'Black Angel' who lived in Pedvin Street (every item she wore was black — gloves, stockings etc. and never any different). Another lady, I can't recall the name she was known by, but always in summer and winter wore heavy dark clothes and a large fur coat. To the other extreme 'Colonel Forty' who lived nearby at Cambridge Park, wore shirt sleeves and summer shorts all through the year and swam regularly summer and winter in the tiny harbour at Salerie Corner.

Two ex-road sweepers we remember, Billy New, a cheery soul always ready to smile and chat. He had a deformed foot and wore one boot built up to help his walk. Mr. John Brache has recently passed away but was always a familiar figure sweeping the 'Town'. Everyone knew him as 'Daisy' as he always wore a large artificial daisy in his hat.

I suppose the most well-known character around St. Peter Port and who is no longer with us was Billy Rowsell — always cheerful and wanting a kiss from all the ladies he knew every time he met them. He sold newspapers — so one always knew he'd catch us in the town. All harmless fun as he was well in his eighties and was living in a 'Hostel' in St. Julian's Avenue. Always he'd say 'I'm coming to your house for tea, and although the invite was there (and from my mother), he'd never come, but it kept him happy to a ripe old age. Around our district we still have one spritely gentleman who has a tremendous memory from many years ago and he goes very much into details and depth of those bygone days — he is always seeking a good listener (even holiday-makers!) and will hold one back if he hasn't finished what he wanted to say! We all admire our Freddie Penney and sincerely hope he shall keep up his actions and conversations for many years to come as long, as he doesn't catch me too often! As I recall Freddie is the last, no-one else comes to mind except for Guernsey's 'Bill' Green — everyone knows Bill on the island but even with his life story in 'Guernsey Green' there is more to it I'm sure!

Sadly though there doesn't seem to be the characters in Town now and nor does there seem to be the 'country folk' talking away in Guernsey patois. It was always lovely listening and hearing them and watching their expressions. Especially on Fridays and Saturdays when the country people came in to shop and meet on those busy market days. The town was full of characters and very crowded and busy, now I only seem to hear the patois being spoken at the 'Viaer Marchi' — A grand annual 'Market' and display of 'old' crafts etc. held at Saumarez Park in aid of the National Trust, or at our own 'Olde Guernsey Market' when we have the Guernsey Dancers performing during the summer evenings. Much enjoyed by everyone with holiday-makers joining in the fun.

The patois or Guernsey French seems to be gradually dying out now and unfortunately it does not get taught in our schools. Still in the country it is spoken amongst the older people but I often wonder how many young people and children can relate to their parents and grandparents. Very few people can speak it in the town and St. Peter Port area — our family never did and of course André's family only spoke the good French.

What did surprise me as regards to our 'patois' was a mention in a book I have read recently written by a G. W. Hugo (born in the year 1862) and called 'Guernsey as it used to be'. He writes 'Patois was generally spoken amongst the Guernsey people until I reached the age of 20 (1882). The chattering of tongues on Saturdays was deafening in the Fish Market, so much so I hated to pass through it'!

A typical sentence he might have heard then and now — 'Cor dammie La! That Molly she goes rabbiting on and on, don't she eh?! Mind you, mon vieux she's hopin' you're enjoying the readin cos there's more to come, she's got a lot to say, eh mon vieux?'

I expect you've noticed that 'eh' and 'me' are very important words used at the end of sentences eh? Also another favourite 'is it?' The next little story brought a different word which could have brought problems!

These past three years André and I had no interest in going away until recently when we decided to resume a rather special friendship with a Portuguese couple. This holiday was a sad reminder of our markets of old — so full of people, the bustle and talking of everyone and the great atmosphere amongst so many stalls full of lovely fresh fruits and vegetables — plus plenty fish of course! Quite an experience which our holiday-makers of old used to enjoy so much and of the market which we locals were so proud of. Sadly like everywhere else I expect the super-markets have taken over, but being in the Algarve again it was Guernsey 20 and 30 years ago as I remember. It was on a visit 12 years ago and our very first visit, when before breakfast I would either swim or take a walk across the sands which to me was the nicest time of day. I could always be guaranteed of meeting usually just one person — a Portuguese man and his little dog walking. He spoke very good English and very soon our conversation was more than a 'good-morning' and a pat on 'Chips' head. 'Chips' was so called because he was found eating chips and was a stray at their home in 'Oporto' — north Portugal. We soon became friends and André and I were given lifts in 'José' and Ericena's car to the markets and the Town. We have since spent probably eight visits in the same area and always these friends (who spend the month of March at their rented apartment) will always get in touch and want to spend days taking us to different parts of the Region. José and Ericena Bandiera are happy, sincere and very kind friends — after three years not seeing them it has given us all a lot of pleasure being together again. José still walks the same beach but with another dog now, called 'Pony' a spaniel as Chips has passed on. Amongst many laughs this year — André ordered our usual drinks at a Café and as always wanting Galeo's (coffee in a glass) — but José heard the pronouncing of the word and told us all these past years we've been ordering COCK-BIRDS! No wonder we've had funny looks!

I'm sure you've gathered that my grandfather Joe Collins was also a character. He was a carpenter by trade but later in life he worked at the 'Banana Market' at Harry Marks along the South Esplanade. Whilst working there he found a tarantula in a box of bananas — it was very large and was taken to be on show in London Museum. He just loved telling tales of years before and seeing André was a good listener would tell the same tales over and over again. Every evening during our courting days! He was a very healthy strong man — we're positive it was the warm fire he sat by *every* evening, his old smelly pipe and his mighty tot of rum that kept him going! He was very contented and a marvel too, he lived until he was almost 95 and could read every word on any newspaper and would never miss an article on the Guernsey Evening Press, all without spectacles — never did he have need to wear glasses.

After the Occupation he didn't seem to take up his old hobby of shooting rabbits etc. but for many years took another hobby. Until his death be raised funds for the Dr. Barnardos Childrens Homes, the British Red Cross Society and the Dogs for the Blind Association. Usually twice a day (at least once) he would take a stroll through the town and also down to the harbour. He would have a chat with the drivers of the lorries waiting to dispatch tomatoes — now in full flow from 1946 onwards. All the men knew him of course and knew he was saving silver paper to send away. This 'job' was to check in all the roadside bins and take out the empty cigarette cartons and collect the silver paper that the cigarettes were wrapped up in. Several times visitors would spot him and think 'poor old chap' and then gladly would give him either one cigarette, but also full packets too! These would then come to my father who did smoke. Mind you I think dad deserved a little reward now and again because he and mum were so patient with Gramp and his paper! Our living room/dining room/lounge although large was always cluttered up around his chair by the fire and always looked like an export depot. Grandpa had three very old heavy-flat irons to flatten the paper and it was always perfectly done. The paper was then packed full to the brim in large tea chests and many many chests were sent away. Everyone in the neighbourhood and even from the country saved and also brought in what they had collected to 'Pop' and he helped raise an awful lot of money for these charities. My mother and father just accepted how he wanted to help and really encouraged him to do so, it became more of a business to him than a hobby and I can never remember a cross word between any of them and Gramp lived with mum and dad until his death in 1962.

At his funeral he was remembered by many, and also a beautiful wreath was sent from 'The Liberation Boys'. These 'boys' together with their families had kept in touch and had spent many happy holidays staying with us all after the war ended.

The States of Guernsey sent an official invitation to a privileged few and Gramp was honoured to be presented to Princess Margaret at Saumarez Park on Tuesday, June 23rd 1959.

Gramp talking to Princess Margaret

CHAPTER 10

NOW A GOOD MOVE TO 'WOODCOTE'

We moved from 'Rosedale' in 1968 after living there for (again) seven years, like we had lived at 'Mon Reve.' Whilst loving the house, it was situated on a very dangerous corner and we were always concerned for the children's safety with fast traffic whizzing around the corner, and really for ours also. So it was decided between us all, to move and for dad to sell the property. We then moved and lived temporarily with mum and dad whilst looking for another house.

Sally and Carole loved the move down to 'Rose Villa' but were most unhappy with a very large old oil painting dad had bought at one of the many auction sales which were held frequently above his building store in Bosq Lane. The painting was of a naval man in costume of many years ago with a ring on his finger with prominent initials plain to see. The girls were positive his eyes moved and followed them upstairs when they went up to their bedrooms and then would lower as they came down. All the four grandchildren of mum and dad were a bit scared of this man and strangely enough André and I have remembered since visiting somewhere (but can't remember where) and a painting such as this being shown to us by a guide. It really did happen! We did all tease dad about his 'finds' — he was always coming in with some 'old junk' as mum would call it. Mostly he would buy very old war weapons, really dangerous looking items which he proudly hung right up the staircase — the oil painting being near the attic bedrooms. He always treasured these 'bargains' and warned us if we laughed he'd never share with us his fortune when he sold them for thousands!

It was not through any sales I assure you but we were lucky as with mum and dad's financial help we had also managed to save a little. Living at Rosedale we had paid dad 10/- rent a week and with taking guests at approximately £1 a day for bed, breakfast and evening meal, we actually managed to buy a small secondhand Austin car and our own bank balance got to four figures! I can remember and smile

Dad and Mum

thinking of our Aunty Edie's (see later) name for us — joking and teasing — 'How's the four figure family then?' She was very pleased for us and proud too of our great achievement as it took us a very long time saving to get there.

Aunty Edie and mum always happy together

When knowing 'Woodcote' was for sale, my first impression of it was not good. It was situated in the right area — Les Canichers and almost opposite Rose Villa, but the kitchen was mainly under the road and not at all convenient. We decided to think about it and the friends wanting to sell who lived at Woodcote at the time gave us until the end of the month to decide. I thought maybe the kitchen could be altered to a utility room; and on the road level a bathroom and lobby could be altered to become our kitchen. Right! We had made up our minds, but we were in for a surprise as an Englishman had pestered the owners into wanting it and they had decided to accept a deposit from him before the end of the month was up. We obviously kicked ourselves for not deciding earlier. Anyway, the owners wanted us to have the property so we were able (under the Property Laws) to repay and reimburse the amount of the deposit paid. We were later told that another property was bought quickly by the gentleman concerned. Now, with again financial and practical help from mum and dad we set about decorating and altering our new home hopefully to accept guests for the 1969 holiday season. Our elderly English friends had originally lived for many years at the house and it badly needed modernisation. We could see it had potential for taking guests and with lovely sea views in three bedrooms, we were encouraged to get busy. Again, dark brown paint everywhere so coats and coats of white paint were to be used. This was to be an upside down house! Uncommon in those days when we thought of the alteration, but now of course are very popular. The family slept in the downstairs rooms overlooking the garden. The sea, harbour and island views were enjoyed by the guests sleeping upstairs. After much hard work we started the season late, but welcomed our first guests by late June. My mother and father were very pleased we lived so close and although they helped me at 'Rosedale' when they could, it was so much easier and handy to pop over and peel potatoes, wash up dishes or iron sheets! During the three years we were living so close, dad would pop over and warn me that the Mail Boat was coming in — 'Look out Mol, the door bell will be ringing soon,' and sure enough, so many weary travellers with suitcases looking for accommodation. It was not unusual to have a dozen or more everyday during the height of the season wanting rooms, not only British. The arrival of the Sark boat brought in the 'one nighters'. Unfortunately we could not help them all but sent them or telephoned other guesthouses to see if they could offer rooms. At one time we could count 12 guesthouses operating in Les Canichers but sadly now only one hotel is open. Also I well remember a grocery shop, a radio shop and a little tiny sweet shop (in the narrow Canichers run by Miss Stacey) also a gents barber (uncle Claude)! all doing well along here when in business. Sadly, all is changed. Nearby the 'Truchot' and 'La Plaiderie', going past the Lower Canichers has altered so much too. We remember the tiny cottages there and the elderly ladies who lived in these terraced little places — always gazing into the large windows to admire the different vases of flowers and ornaments on display — always a pleasure walking into town. For this year I have decided to offer again B&B and also a self catering unit as I have always loved meeting and seeing guests around. I think mainly it is because I am proud of being 'Guernsey' and have loved showing and talking about our Island. Mum and dad felt the same, with many happy hours talking to guests. The one time I used to look forward to and love to remember was, after preparing and serving the evening meal — it was then the 'staff coffee time' — André, dad, (sometimes mum) and myself. Knowing the guests had had their fill and were happy talking together, we'd sit in the kitchen and just chat. There was no rush for visitors to move from the table or for dad to rush home. It is strange that it is the ordinary 'together' times that to me were the happiest. It is like remembering the family get together always for Sunday lunch. My sister and family and us also, would (if we had no guests), enjoy our Sunday roasts with mum and dad. We still carry on the 'old tradition' with our family now and I hope these special couple of hours together will always be remembered for the happy times by all the family, even when our grandchildren have grown up.

Sadly, dad passed away in 1972, aged 68 years so we only enjoyed him close by for three years, but it was a blessing then for mum that we had decided to live close by. For dad too, having retired almost 10 years before with ill health, our home and the guests must have given him new interests and much pleasure.

CHAPTER 11

HAVING DAUGHTERS!

The girls were growing up and with encouragement did help, a little! I don't think they were overkeen but understood the guests did pay towards keeping a car and the annual holidays we began to take in 1972 — our first being to Jersey and taking mum with us. The girls were also able to take a holiday abroad with their schools. It was quite something special then to travel to a foreign land when aged 12 and 13 years old. Sally (the elder) joined a school cruising holiday from Guernsey and it was probably due to enjoying this holiday that when she was 18 years old a longer stay much further afield was planned. Sally was a shorthand typist at 'Kleinwort Benson' at the time, when she came home one day saying her good friend and colleague Beverley James had the opportunity of going to South Africa for six months and would be staying with an 'Aunt and Uncle'. I felt Sally was putting out feelers so to speak but did not say too much, just waited! We did not have to wait too long as within the next day or two Sally quite casually asked 'Would you mind very much mum and dad if I went to South Africa with Bev?' My thoughts went back a few years then as I remember very well my great friend Irene (whom I worked with) and I asking my mother if she would mind very much if we joined the W.R.A.F. At that time (three or four years after the War ended), we had got a bit bored with the Telephone Exchange and having both stayed in Guernsey throughout the Occupation we would have liked to see a little of the world. All seemed very glamorous to us at the time. We were aged 18 and 19, the same ages as Sally and Beverley. Well on asking my mother — within seconds she was very tearful saying 'Well, you can go, but I've brought you up respectful for 18 years and now you want to leave us etc., etc, but yes you can go!' Dad was all for us going but seeing mum like this and the reaction we had, left me in no doubt and nothing more was said. It is a nice feeling now to think my sister and I did not cause any undue worry to mum and dad at this time. We were both working in St Peter Port and living at home. We were the best of friends and pals and had the same interests, being members of Ebenezer Church, the choir, the Sunday School and Girls' Life Brigade. Later we married within two months of each other which I expect looking back now must have been a wrench and in a way a little sad. We only moved to homes in St Peter Port though and with our four children being all born more or less the same time, they all grew up together and gave mum and dad a lot of pleasure. We were a close family.

Now back to Sally and it's surprising how you can get a turn around as one gets older and it was myself and André's turn to get a little sinking feeling in the tummy. Thinking it was really an opportunity not to be missed, there was no real hesitation on our part although we felt she was still too young to go and six months seemed a long time to be away.

As it happened, we had met an English lady and her husband (a South African) from Pretoria the year before and who had been guests in our home. A very nice couple, and they were living quite near to Mr. and Mrs. Ogier (Beverley's friends known to her as aunt and uncle), so we felt we had a contact we could rely on. So really we were pleased for the girls and with much confidence they bought their six month return tickets hoping they would find work on arrival. It was not as easy as they thought it would be, but it was again fortunate we had met this couple Marjorie and Phillip Nel, as Phillip worked as an official at the 'Government Office' so he was in a position to pull a few strings and get the girls a work permit. This normally takes months but they had theirs within two weeks and within a week after they began work together at the Barclays National Bank. Luckily they had an advantage as their work previously in Guernsey was dealing in 'Foreign Exchange'. Unfortunately their stay at Mr. and Mrs. Ogier did not work out too well so they moved into a small boarding or lodging house, as they are called there. They enjoyed everything in South Africa, especially the many friends they made and the fascinating journey they had taken through the 'garden route' to Table Mountain at Capetown.

Arriving back looking themselves like Africans and sounding like them too, they had plenty to say and it was lovely having them back again safe and sound, no matter what age one still worries over one's children!

The following year Sally again got the travel bug and she wanted to work and learn conversational German amongst the people. She applied for a job advertised in an Austrian Hotel. To be a chambermaid amazed us! Although being involved with guests at home it was certainly going to be different working at it all day. Especially so in a foreign country and not knowing anything of the language, but she was ready for a change again and was quite confident to go on her own. Well, this hotel in Kitzbuhel was a fairly large hotel and very busy. She had not realised she'd have to work so hard, especially having to wash down balconies and blinds *everyday*, cleaning windows and never thought rooms could be left so untidy, *everyday*! Plus beds, beds and more bed-making *everyday*! Saying all that she must have done well as the management wanted her to return for the winter (and busier season) — she declined — thank you very much, as although her intentions were to learn the German language she was working with Yugoslav women who spoke neither English or German!

Carole our younger daughter also travelled with a school party to Switzerland. Then at the Grammar School she attended, pupils were asked to join an exchange system with Austrian pupils. We thought this a good idea and encouraged Carole to join also. Arrangements were made for 'Sylvia' to come to Guernsey first for a holiday after Carole had corresponded with her for a while. Sylvia was the same age as Carole, 12 years old, but we could hardly believe this when we first saw her at the airport. She was head and shoulders above Carole almost 6ft and a real beauty. She could easily have been a fashion model with a beautiful figure too. Sylvia spoke good English and settled in with us very well. She also loved the English cooking and at meal times — Carole and Sylvia would chant at the kitchen table 'Wir haben hunger — hunger haben wir' — you can maybe guess — 'we have hunger, hunger have we' and so Sylvia tucked in with a very hearty appetite. It was good to see her eat and enjoy the food but then she enjoyed everything about the Island and she returned again. When Carole did the 'exchange' and left for Austria, she was escorted and looked after by the Austrian Society and went to stay with Sylvia's parents, Mr. and Mrs. Jablonski. They ran a butcher's shop in Vienna and worked many hours all day and every day and lived in a flat nearby. Carole enjoyed the first visit and went also for a second visit, this time to stay with Sylvia and a group of friends in a mountain village called 'Hans'. Sylvia skied expertly, Carole couldn't of course. So Sylvia used to carry her on her back when skiing down the long slopes!

Carole had always wanted to train and qualify as a psychiatric nurse but with a little persuasion from us decided to try for her general nursing first. Because of her love for Guernsey and the sea, she tried for and was accepted to train at Poole and the surrounding districts. We had not realised (neither had she told us) but it only has been fairly recently that we found out how very homsesick she had been after leaving the Island. There was no training facilities in Guernsey for 'SRN' then. We welcomed her home as often as we could and when her free time would allow but I never really got used to saying

'Goodbye' to her each time at the airport. André and I did miss her very much and also missed her young friends popping in. After three years training she passed her nursing exam and we travelled to Dorchester and felt very proud when she stepped up for her award at the presentation.

Carole worked at Christchurch Hospital for a year then came home and had to wait five or six weeks for a vacancy to come up at Guernsey's Princess Elizabeth Hospital. Although enjoying her work she never really settled as she never forgot her ambition to work for the R.M.N. (Registered Mental Nurse) qualification. She began writing again and was accepted at Exeter to start training at Exe Vale Hospital, Exminster. The room she was given to occupy was certainly an eye opener, so tiny, bare and cold. It was really dreadful and when I saw it my heart sank. It was a disgrace for these young people to have to live in such rooms — which really reminded me of prison cells without the bars.

They also had to work in a very large old building — (hospital now has been closed) so drab, dark and having to work and look after very mentally ill patients. No comfort at all, so we wanted Carole to find somewhere to live privately which would be suitable and rent reasonable. At first she shared a house with two nursing friends, then took on a nice flat on her own. Although she was a very sensible and confident girl in her early 20s we still worried about her. Don't we always?

You may remember in 'A Child's War', I mentioned Carole was living on a boat (what freedom!). Well, she learned to sail whilst she was living and training at Exeter and a very competent yachtsman(?) she turned out to be. On gaining her R.M.N. qualification after 18 months training she wanted a break from it and took a job teaching students and families to sail during the summer season on the River Dart. A beautiful part of the country, very picturesque and ideal for boating. She lived on the 30' yacht 'Delphinus' but unfortunately she had many problems with it. Although she was earning when the yacht wasn't under repairs, like all boats the cost of keeping it was too expensive. At the end of the season Carole decided she would bring back Delphinus to Guernsey on her own! Then I did well and truly begin to worry. She sensed this and eventually gave in to our suggestion that she have company bringing the boat back. Sally's husband Michael and his father John Howlett (who also loves the sea and boats) would fly over and join Carole to bring the yacht over. I really thought at long last Carole would be home for good and would settle to nursing at the Castel Hospital. She enjoyed taking friends out sailing, unfortunately some got very sea sick even before they had set sail and we had a rough sail once! Carole loved the time she spent on

Delphinus and it gave her a lot of enjoyment. She travelled as far as Jersey and to Alderney and then to Cherbourg and back on her own, after staying three nights in Alderney with no problems at all and four in Cherbourg. She was a slim built girl but very determined in everything she wanted to do. So much so when her boy friend from Exeter wanted her to travel back to Dartmouth she was all for going alone, but as it turned out, in very worrying conditions. She left the house at 9 a.m. to get everything prepared ready for her journey and we wished her 'Bon Voyage' yet again. It wasn't until I drove to the west coast at Cobo Bay in the afternoon did I realise how very strong the wind was with very rough seas and plenty of 'white horses'. On returning home at 5 p.m. I telephoned the Signal Station and asked what time 'Delphinus' had left and whether there was any news of her. The signalman told me the yacht had left for Jersey(!) during the late morning and there was a lone young man sailing her!! It took some convincing on my part to tell him it was our daughter on board and she was heading for Dartmouth! André and I were very concerned on hearing this and tried the ship to shore telephone to reach her. When eventually hearing her tiny voice and the wind howling and waves lashing, I began to panic, wouldn't you? We could not hear her properly above the noise of sea and wind and all I remember saying was 'come back as soon as you can and we'll ring the Signal Station' — silence — we just did not know where she was nor whether she'd get back in one piece.

At 9.00 a.m. apparently the weather forecast had been good and the wind was due to drop during the afternoon but instead the wind had made Force 8 or 9! To make matters worse, due to the strong tides running she had to sail around to the south of the Island before heading north towards the mainland. Normally one would set sail northwards all along the east coast then towards and passing Alderney. So instead, she had to sail around St. Martin's Point, around Pleinmont before heading north. As the tides were, she reached the Hanois Lighthouse and tried to get around it, but just couldn't with such heavy swells in the gale and the many currents to contend with. She didn't want to give in, but after a few hours and hearing our concern she had to reluctantly turn back to St. Peter Port. At the end of the Pierheads we were so relieved to see a couple of bobbly lights nearing and realised it was our 'Cas' and Delphinus making for home.

It is strange and funny to think back now but when Carole was a little girl (and as a toddler) she always chatted to an imaginary friend by her side. 'Captain' or 'Capn' she called him and he was a Captain from a boat and this imaginary friend was really with her for years. A letter she wrote also as a little girl saying she was going to travel the world with her 'Captain' on his boat. Maybe she will one day as she

MUM! HAVE YOU MADE THE SOUP YET?

eventually went back to Dartmouth and married her 'Capn' Geoff Cottam — who had also taught her to sail and who had run the 'Blue Seas Sailing School' at Dartmouth for many years. With all her and his sailing experience (RYA/DTP Yachtsmaster Instructor) and having written a successful large instructive book on sailing (Fast Facts!) one wonders if dreams will come true one day. Carole and Geoff married in 1987 (March 19) and lived on the mainland at Dartmouth and Totnes for 2½ years. They have two lovely children now, Joshua 4½ years and Naomi 2 years old and now living in Guernsey.

Sally's (our elder daughter) husband Michael Howlett and his father John jointly own a 45' fishing boat called 'Starlight'. (GU 194). It is a job which takes them out together fishing and trawling off the Islands all through the night and all day for long periods if the sea is calm and the tides are not too high. During winter it can be a lean time as the seas around our Island can be very unkind to fishermen (also to travellers on the not so modern boats of years ago — Dad was at one time the 'States' Diver and would retrieve many items from the sea bed including many sets of false teeth!).

Sally and Michael live in Guernsey and they also have two lovely children (aren't all grandchildren?) There's Ryan aged 10 and Carly almost eight but I doubt whether Ryan will follow in dad's footsteps although he also loves the sea and boats and football! This summer he is hopeful to see the dolphins at play around 'Starlight' with his dad and grandpa (like they were during the 1991 summer). Carly will be pleased for him to take a trip as (like she says) she can have some peace then. We have been most fortunate in many ways having the 'Howletts' live at Rose Villa the family home opposite for eleven years since their marriage. Whenever I look across at the house I can still see Ryan sitting as a toddler on the window sill till late evening watching the boats instead of sleeping!

The Cottams also on leaving the mainland lived entirely with André and I at Woodcote for two years, now gladly for both families in September 1991 they both have settled in nice homes and are happy in them. Carole and Geoff (both Christians) give up a lot of their time encouraging and helping, especially young men in their Church work. Both our daughters and the four grandchildren have given André and I lots of pleasure, also to my mother. There is a bond and something very close, loving and natural between the very young and the very old. I've seen it so often in my mother's face and in the children's — playing simple games together be it snap, ludo or just enjoying colouring books together. A real joy to us all.

'The Cottams'. Naomi and Joshua

'The Howletts'
Carly and Ryan.
Our daughters Sally and Carole showed independence when younger and did well.
They are now happily married to Michael and Geoffrey.
André and I are very proud of them all.

CHAPTER 12

BARE BOTTOMS AND BARE BOOBS!

Whilst living at Woodcote for over 23 years and seven years previously at Rosedale, we have accommodated many people from many different walks of life. Prison officers (from Dartmoor), doctors, policemen, many 'British Rail' workers, custom officers and even to a famous TV star! This reminds me of the time when the dining room was sorting out the best plan for a couple to take an expensive gold ring away after buying that day — not knowing a Customs Officer was sitting amongst them! We met every nationality. Looking back with happy memories at my visitors book, we had guests stay with us mostly from the mainland but also from Ireland and much further afield — from Australia, New Zealand, America, Canada, Holland, Israel, regulars from Sweden usually twice a year and from Germany, South Africa, Andorra, France, Denmark, Finland, Switzerland, Norway, Italy and Jersey!!

Of course with most nationalities there were bound to be some language problems — but again there are always 'vays and means'! André helped quite a bit with the French as he talks and understand very well but I don't! German was my better subject at school and this was useful also. We had a Frenchman stay, a Mons. Derrier who was a chef! He couldn't speak any English at all but he always wanted to know what kind of soup he was having. The first night I told him 'chicken noodle' — he looked puzzled so I chanted and raised my voice 'Cocka doodle doo' (with expression of course!). He smiled and understood. Oh dear, I dreaded the next evening's explanation, it was to be oxtail — so can you imagine the laughter in the Dining Room when I wiggled my hand towards my rear mooing very loudly when doing so. I was grateful Mons. Derrier although a nice man was on a short visit! I'm afraid André wasn't too helpful at these times, he just kept in the kitchen and laughed at my antics. We really had many laughs with guests, especially making an effort in dressing up, say in our red, white and blue for special celebrations. May 9th (again!) our special day was enjoyed always by our guests and another day springs to mind when Prince Charles and Lady Diana were married. All the guests joined in and dressed up for breakfast in red, white and blue. We all had a wonderful time — a party breakfast! and the guests did not mind me serving breakfasts in a flowery red white and blue hat (at least it did not put them off their hearty platefuls!).

Our friends Mr. and Mrs. Chaciewitz who ran the 'Sardrette' Hotel opposite us asked us one day if I could help them by accommodating nine or ten people. A fishing party from Jersey for a couple of nights? they asked. Yes, I could manage this, so being prepared waited for the party. Dad was in the kitchen with me when we heard a loud sound of heavy boots as if marching ('sounds like Jerries again' I said to dad) — then there was a commotion at the door and when I opened it facing me were (it seemed like) 20 soldiers! 'We've booked with you' they said. 'Oh no, I'm waiting for a fishing party from Jersey,' then laughs all round. 'It's us, we're the demolition party from Jersey.' They had joined the Jersey Territorial Army and had an exercise planned in Guernsey, and returned to stay with us many times after this visit. A nice lot of lads again with many laughs especially so when I found a little yellow plastic duck in the bathroom. You can imagine the teasing amongst the 'privates' when they found out it belonged to the Sergeant in charge — his little play toy for the bath!

At Woodcote — formerly called 'Rose Adele' like I mentioned is an upsidedown house. We have a bridge running from road to front entrance door (houses are all built similarly in Les Canichers) and in the courtyard below under the flagstones is a very large cistern holding almost 4,000 gallons of water. Under the 'utility' room below the road is a very deep well and we also have a large cellar which runs the full length of the house. It is much larger than its front appearance. The kitchen now has changed to road level with also the dining room and lounge. Visitors' bedrooms were downstairs and upstairs. We and the girls slept downstairs so it was really not surprising a few guests did get confused, especially those from America! They were an elderly couple who arrived late afternoon, after a cup of tea they must have dozed off and the dinner gong aroused them. They were convinced it was breakfast time and were very confused and disorientated at this time. Anyway, after a meal they seemed brighter and chatted to other guests in the lounge. I went to bed around 10.30 p.m. trying always to keep to this time ready for the early morning rise — I was enjoying a little read before André came down and heard him come into the room, or so I thought! But surprise, surprise, it was our American friend all ready to jump into bed! I, again took him and showed him his room upstairs and then decided to find out where his wife was. She was sound asleep in the lounge but when awakened she was asking for her breakfast! It took this elderly couple two days to really settle in and lose the 'jet lag', but by this time their flying visit was over and they were due to fly to the mainland and then home again.

There were embarrassing times also but having dealings with guests at all times, it could not be avoided. One gentleman wanted milk brought to him early in the morning. After the second morning I decided to leave the milk outside the door because when I had knocked and he opened the door, I was confronted by a mirror on my right showing our guest's bare bottom! What a sight first thing in the morning!

Now I can't keep telling stories of other people when I do silly things myself can I? This is a little embarrassing thing that happened whilst on holiday with our good friends Ben and Sylvia Hervé — they delight in telling their friends and why not if it causes a laugh? We were in self catering apartments in Tenerife and at that time (a few years ago), Sylvia was trying to get me to sunbathe topless which I was adamant I wouldn't. No coaxing would have made me. Well after lunch one day André was having a snooze on the balcony and I also had been sunbathing in a two piece costume. Seeing the gentleman on the balcony next to ours I decided to stand and have a chat and looking down towards the 'pool' spotted Sylvia and Ben — we smiled and waved, then Sylvia stood up and seemed to be pointing down on herself. This puzzled me, as she continued to do so with more emphasis towards herself, she was really laughing now and Ben also, plus friends joined in. I remarked to the gent 'I really don't know what my friends are trying to tell me' — he kept silent — but suddenly it dawned on me and I looked down on myself, yes you've guessed it — one in and one out! Oh dear, was my face red as I turned away and looked down again at them giggling at the poolside. So much for 'modest Mol'!!

Irene is another 'friend' who lets me down! She remembers the time I retraced my steps to all shops I'd visited in the Town looking for a headscarf I'd lost. In the last shop I was explaining it was pink with a sort of 'clock' on it — the assistant looked at me and said 'Is it like the one on your head?' Enough said, but there's more!!

Back to guests and there were a couple of instances which caused some concern — again we consider ourselves very fortunate not to have had more. The Tourist Office telephoned asking me to accommodate two people. When they arrived they were men working on the Island. It was only luck I had asked where they were working but unlucky for one! They booked in for three nights and the first morning only one came down for breakfast early and went off — the second bed had not been slept in. The next morning the rather sheepish looking guest only wanted early tea and went off. He told me not to disturb his colleague as he wanted to sleep on — I noted he went off with a smallish red suitcase. It was Sunday and by noon I decided to wake up the other guest. I was not at all surprised to find no-one in bed and on checking the bed that had been slept on was disgusted to find it soaking wet right through the candlewick, blankets, sheets to mattress! Not very nice and I knew then we would not be seeing either men return. After our lunch André and I decided to make our way to the Company where I remembered one said they would be working, fitting carpets. Off we set and sure enough outside the warehouse was a carpet company van and the familiar red suitcase laying underneath. We called out, banged on the door for several minutes but no answer at all. I wanted to grab the suitcase and take it home but André thought it best to return home and call in the police. We explained everything to them and they said 'leave it to us'. Come 10 p.m. and a ring at the door, our sheepish little man stood there between two policemen. They called me to one side and said he'd reported his suitcase missing (funny it was at the station!!) and besides having hundreds of pounds on him he also had a key for a room booked at the Old Government House Hotel for the night! The police told me to charge for everything — full accommodation for both men, plus all laundry *and* a new mattress! I couldn't bring myself to charge all they suggested but maybe this episode taught him a lesson. The police said they knew these characters only too well but always they continue trying it on.

The only other time when two couples tried to get away without paying was also on a short visit and had come on 'spec' so to speak. I came in from the garden to find a note on the telephone 'Have decided to spend the weekend in Jersey — will be back on Monday to settle up!' That wasn't good enough I thought, so I telephoned the hire car company and funnily enough they had doubts about these characters also. They had known they were going to Jersey and had already alerted the Jersey Police. I felt I just had time to make it to the 'Condor' before she left the harbour and luckily as I left the house a friend was passing in her car. 'Jump in' she said and within two minutes we were there. I was allowed on board even though 'Condor' was ready to leave.

As I entered I saw the couple and straightaway they recognised me, stood up and took their wallets from their back pockets. They were absolutely bulging with notes, hundreds of pounds but gladly a few pounds less after my visit. How they got on in Jersey I do not know.

We soon forgot these instances as everyone seemed to love their holiday here — all with different hobbies or things to do. One gentleman who came with his wife every year from Birmingham spent his holiday fishing at the end of Castle Walk on the harbour pier every day! Another younger man from London exercised every morning before breakfast and ran and jogged as far as Petit Bot or L'Ancresse and back again every day. You can guess for yourself the size breakfast he needed afterwards!

Talking of exercise and fishing, one family booked in and coming downstairs after arriving, the gent held back for a chat. He was middle-aged and had immediately changed into running shorts and started jogging on the spot whilst chatting to me. He said he had to keep up with his son who was running in the forthcoming Commonwealth Games. The guest now intended to run to St. Sampsons and back! With that he proudly said he'd recently had an operation on the tummy and pulling down his shorts wanted me to see the scar! Oh dear — I thought we're in for some fun here. Not only did I have a little laugh and some fun with this very nice gentleman, but so did a few children. They had gathered at Beau Sejour (Cambridge Park) when he went there with his long fishing rod and practised casting off! Can you imagine the puzzled looks and the giggles of the children who gathered around to see this unusual sight!

Regular guests (although with no real menu) would either hint or I just knew of their favourite food — like 'spotted dick' and 'bread pudding'. I don't think I ever disappointed the 'special' guests of ours who called themselves 'The Three Puds'! At times there would be a commotion in the Dining Room with more than one wanting the bottom 'second' portion of the sherry trifle or the rice pudding basin. I knew my guests and among my regular ones I must mention the 'Kelly Clan' — a special family who still holiday in Guernsey year after year and have done for the past 46 years. The Mother, Gran and Great Gran of the family was Florence Kelly (Aunty Flo to us and to many) — a very dear lady who was Guernsey born and who had eight children. Before the war being married to an English soldier they could only visit very occasionally her beloved Guernsey. After the war, she and her husband Colin started coming again and by then bringing their unmarried children — eventually all marrying and still all visiting and loving Guernsey. My father was a cousin to aunty Flo so the family were always accommodated (somehow) at 'Rose Villa'. Every year at least eight or nine descended on my mother and gradually the overspill came to me when living at 'Woodcote'.

By now the children had married and babies were coming along and any number between 14 and 24 wanted to come! With the larger numbers coming guest houses nearby took all those that we couldn't and we usually managed to give them an evening meal altogether as a family, just what they wanted. With the guest houses closing nearby and with so many wanting to come at the same time and every year — they now (although fewer at eight to 10) stay at a smaller comfortable hotel with a bar and swimming pool. These eight just would not miss their annual holiday in the Island even though some years they try other places. At the 'Olde Guernsey Market' on Thursdays I'm very happy hearing of guests like the 'Kellys' who return year after year and to know they think of Guernsey as 'Home from Home' and still a friendly Island.

I should love to mention many by name whom we have met during our 27 years in business, but I would have to miss so many out. With my mother's popularity and whilst she was alive we received always over 300 Christmas cards from relatives, friends and visitors. It proved how so many visitors want to keep in touch as most enclosed a little family newsletter for the year. Although tiring answering back to all these good people who wrote, what a great satisfaction André and I have had over the years.

André, mum and I with guests at Woodcote

For many years when mum was younger she was employed as an excellent and efficient waitress. She worked at different large functions and used to teach, organise and book the ladies for these dinners and lunches. Mum had also the honour of serving on the Queen (then as Princess Elizabeth, with the Duke of Edinburgh) during visits to the Island. Always loving the work mum was always a great help to me and used to cheerfully wait on the tables. Many guests remember the pleasant times with her and the laughs — she had many tales to tell and many expressions she showed when telling stories of the Occupation. Visitors enjoyed many happy evenings with mum and with dad too. Many a time the guests would be invited over the road to her home then 'Rose Villa' and after a chat she would sit at her large piano and play brilliantly doing all the necessary actions. This impressed our friends very much until they realised it was a 'Pianola' and mum had placed the old tuneful rolls in the piano beforehand, it was all set up for mum to sit and get her legs moving backwards and forwards. She had a couple of hundred rolls many old favourite tunes which had given mum a lot of pleasure since dad was no longer with her. We have always been a family of music lovers and my earliest memories before the war was learning to play the piano. Before I had even begun to learn 'properly' my mother had taught me several tunes and one I remember so well playing with her 'Ain't she sweet'.

My cousin Joan Collins a very attractive and lovely girl — who had been chosen as Miss Guernsey's Beauty Queen before the war and who was a qualified teacher of piano was naturally chosen to teach me. After maybe half a dozen lessons (I was probably seven years old at the time) I was taken for another lesson but on this particular day whilst waiting for Joan I knelt down and patted her large dog (a Borzoi) who was lying on the settee. I must have got too close as he went and bit my nose and I needed three stitches! Joan and family were most upset and although he was a beautiful dog and a pedigree show dog, they had him put to sleep straightaway. My father with his workmen offered to bury it next day. The workmen dug what they thought was a suitable hole for an average dog but all exclaimed and were surprised, as they felt it was the size of a donkey! The dictionary describes a Borzoi as a Russian Wolfhound! Anyway, the incident put paid to my lessons for a while as believe it or not, three weeks after this dog bite, I fell over in the garden and broke my nose!!

Dad had covered a square chimney stack with small pieces of broken china (very decorative like the 'Little Chapel' at Les Vauxbelets) and had placed it by our front door in the garden. Being awkward I fell and caught my nose on the sharp corner. When Dad came home for lunch, he didn't recognise me with my very swollen face and black and blue eyes!

During 1938 the family moved down to the Canichers and for a short while I went for lessons again to a Mrs. Loaring who lived nearby, but really mum and I enjoyed playing the piano by 'ear' and the memory of 'Ain't she sweet' and the tune of it will always remind me of mum. Perhaps the family weren't too impressed with our playing but we thoroughly enjoyed ourselves. When the family on my mother's side of aunts, uncles and many cousins got together at Christmas or at any special time there was always one of the family waiting for their turn to play. Locals will remember the very talented Rex (Collins) who played at many different venues and also of Les (both cousins) who was a number one sportsman on the Island (footballer and C.I. Boxing Champion at one time), made no difference he also had to wait his turn to play the old joanna! Apparently my grandmother whom I don't remember very well (born Kate Mayo in Dorset) mum's mother and Joe's wife was an excellent piano accordionist and played all the time when a younger woman. Also her brothers all played many musical instruments and were professional bandsmen. I'm pleased to say our daughters and grand-daughter Carly also even little Naomi and Joshi seem to have talent and interest too in music. It would be nice to think there could be musical family get together evenings for the future. Let's hope they will come back.

CHAPTER 13

COINCIDENCES AND FRIENDSHIPS!

Since 1985 and 'A Child's War' was printed, I have had many coincidences come to light. First and foremost an unintentional lie I had written which I shall put to rights now. Do you remember me telling you of our black Collie Dog 'Billy' who had been left behind in Alderney when the civilian population left the island at the beginning of the Occupation? He was brought down by Mart Whelan who had to help finally clear the place and who was living with us at Rose Villa at the time. After looking after Billy and generally getting very fond of our new pet, mum told Joyce and I that Billy was hungry and seeing we just couldn't manage to feed him he would have to be sent to Sark where he would be fed better and well looked after. We were very upset but pleased to think he would have more to eat where he was going. Well, during one of our get togethers last year at the Channel Islands Occupation Society outings, I was speaking to Mr. Bill Crawford who used to work for my father all those years before. He was speaking of my parents and especially remarking what a case my mother was — then he happened to say "I'll never forget having to bury that large dog of yours during the Occupation." We never knew our Billy had died. Mum and dad had known Joyce and I would have been upset and there would have been more tears for Billy, so Mr. Crawford and Dad had quietly buried him in a garden in the 'Back Canichers'. Maybe he died through missing his Alderney life and family, or through food shortages, we'll never know, but hopefully it was natural and just due to old age.

Another little story which involves the Island of Alderney. Like Bill Bougourd, there were others (who despite being a very punishable act if caught by the Germans), kept a diary of the day to day happenings during the Occupation of the Island. Now at last! I wasn't imagining this scene of so many years ago. It is only today 4th April 1992 printed in the 'Guernsey Evening Press' I have found my memories were correct! A very interesting wartime diary written by a Methodist

Minister, the Rev. Douglas Ord has after all these years come to light. I remember Rev. Ord very well preaching and taking services at Ebenezer Church and now his diary of the Occupation years has been recognised as a very important record of the war years, and a summary has been printed for all islanders to read. As a girl during the early years I have always pictured and remembered in my mind seeing so many children and grown-ups standing on and sorting through piles of clothes, toys and small items of furniture which filled and were stacked high in the end Children's Bathing Pool at La Valette. The grown ups carried sacks and were loaded up coming away with the goods, some looked desperate sorting out these wet dripping clothes. Before writing 'A Child's War' I had asked numerous 'older' people if they had known or recollected this happening. No-one did and I felt I must have dreamt it, although it has always been clear in my mind and I had always known and wondered why I had always remembered all these items had come down from Alderney?

Anyway, after all this time — Rev. Ord had recorded —

"There was an interesting scene at La Valette on June 28th 1941. About 100 people gathered at the Bathing Pool where they had a busy time salvaging garments brought from Alderney in a verminous condition and dumped into the sea water in the hope that this might cleanse them." Mr. Ord referred to this incident as 'dreadful measures' illustrating the need for clothes.

Although a sad little story thinking of all the Alderney Islanders who had to vacate their homes for the whole Occupation time, I am sure the clothes and goods were very well used and most welcome during this very lean time on our Island.

During this time or most probably later Alderney must have resembled a large prison camp with hundreds of prisoners-of-war of all nationalities, but mainly of Russians and Jews who were cruelly treated, literally starving and who were made to slave and work on the great fortifications. Hundreds of these poor men died as the result.

Mr. Ian Griggs (specialist in the Postal History of the German Occupation of the Channel Islands) has for many years been interested in the S. S. Vega — our life saving ship which brought to the Islands food parcels and commodities through the Red Cross during the latter part of the war when all the Islanders were really starving. These welcome parcels were so precious they were guarded and under supervision all day and night by the Guernsey Police, the German Forces and St. John's Ambulance personnel.

Ian Griggs travelled to many countries researching for a book he is writing of the journeys and all the adventures the 'Vega' has experienced during past years. I happened to be delivering my books at The Guernsey Occupation Museum one day. I was there just a couple of minutes when I overheard a gentleman at the counter enquiring as to whether there were any books printed about the 'Vega'. The assistant naturally said no, he didn't think so. Knowing of the intention of Mr. Grigg's book in the making, I had to mention this to this very nice gentleman. He was then most interested and told us that the Captain at the time of the war on the 'Vega' was his uncle, 'Captain Wideberg'. This gentleman from Sweden — 'Claes Goran Lindstrom' immediately took Ian's name and address and got in touch with him. Of course Ian was very excited about this unexpected meeting and coincidence with a member of the Captain's family and was given much help and information for his forthcoming book. Through this meeting Ian was able to get in touch also with close members of Captain Wideberg's family, together with many photographs of him on his ship. Research by Mr. Griggs is still going on, but hopefully one day we shall read of our beloved Vega's exploits. The parcels and medical supplies etc. meant a happy ending of the Occupation and more than anything else, just knowing we islanders weren't entirely forgotten gave an added boost to life, when everyone was at life's lowest ebb.

On the mainland too, life was not easy with shortages and separation from loved ones and the frightening air raids to contend with. I have received and was interested to read a little of what life was like in Berlin at this time. Mrs. Monika Panning, as you will read wrote to me in 1989 after visiting Guernsey with her husband. Maybe, readers you will be interested too . . .

Hannover   *July 14th, 1989*
Dear Mrs. Bihet,

For the first time September last year my husband and I visited Guernsey. We have learnt to love the island and am back this year for refreshing our English knowledges by private tuition. Going home again I bought your book "A child's war" and today I have finished it, word for word I have read, translated and sought the unknown vocabulary. I have found the reading very interesting and have enjoyed knowing of your life.

There are parallels between us. My husband and I were born 1941 in Berlin, and my family (my husband's family was evacuated) stayed in Berlin during the whole war. I can't remember so much but something you told in your book I have lived to myself.

We were always hungry too. Berlin is a big city and it was very very difficult for my mother to organize our daily food. She went with completely overcrowded trains which departed and arrived at some time or other to the surroundings of Berlin to barter all our linen, china, carpets, jewels, finally the wedding rings of my parents for some potatoes, eggs or vegetables. Often she took along with me, it was a better impression to show the misery with a slim spindly daughter at hand.

I know also like you the deep community to the family, friends and neighbours. We have had nearly nothing and divided this with others.

I have own memories to the allied soldiers, British, American, French and also Russian, who were very often very kindly to children.

I remember only one care parcel we have got from the USA and my first orange which was in it — like you I hadn't a clue to what it tasted like or how I was going to tackle it.

I remember sitting in a pram and my mother walked many hours across the town to visit her parents and parents-in-law, and the buildings and streets were burning. I know the nights in the bunker with many many people and beds one upon another. — My mother and her friend scrounged potatoes like you — once a half bath-tub full.

Unfortunately I have no power of recollection of the day of the end of the war. I was 4 years and 5 months old, too young for a lot of memories.

After the war the only radio station of Berlin was situated in the Russian sector. There I co-operated in the broadcasts for children. For that — it was a good luck — I got beside some money products of nature from the Russians. So I could help to support the family with loaves of white bread I remember, cabbage and so on.

Today I try to help with care-parcels to Romania. It was very difficult to get a private address. Sure you know that the Red Cross couldn't help these poor hungry people. Beside coffee, chocolate and other "luxurious" food I send for instance baking-powder, margarine, oil, tinned meat, beef-cube.

I hope you can understand my letter, excuse me the mistakes. My first and favourite language at school was Latin. Late but I hope not too late I begin to like more and more English. It would be a great pleasure for my husband and me to get to know you. We have thoughts of coming back to Guernsey at September next year.

Sure you can understand now my great interest to your booklet. Thank you you have written it.

Excuse me the incorrect English but by reading your book sure I have learnt a little bit more correct English.

Many greeting for me and my husband.
Monika Panning

There is one elderly gentleman (who since writing to me regularly since early 1987) whom I should very much like to meet again. It was only a brief talk I had with him during a Thursday afternoon whilst I was at my stall at the 'Olde Guernsey Market'. If I remember rightly the first visit he made he did not look too pleased at the 'wares' I was selling. The 'swastika' flag on the front of by book (and others) apparently offend some Germans. This gent stood by and watched, maybe to listen to comments from other people or to his own fellow countrymen. Anyway, lo and behold the next week I noted the same face amongst the crowd of holidaymakers and he came forward. He then did buy my book and told me he was from Germany, which I had already guessed. Within a fortnight this gentleman wrote to me in perfect English and reminded me of the little chat we had had at the market. He was impressed by the way I had written my memories and I suppose pleased I hadn't painted all Germans in a bad light, only as I remembered them as a child. He wanted to write to me as a friend which I agreed to do, and it has turned out by letters I have received from other sources that Erich Wegner was a very brave man during the war and had saved many British lives during a particular naval action off Crete.

Below is a part of a letter sent from the German Erich to a Mr. John Stevens, the President of the 'Fighting G. Club' for the H.M.S. Gloucester survivors. H.M.S. Gloucester was a cruiser of 9600 tons which was sunk on May 22nd 1941 near the Island of Kythera. After seeing an article in 1986 printed in the 'Navy News' seeking the possible whereabouts of any survivors from H.M.S. Gloucester — John wrote to Erich and was most honoured to correspond and hear from him again.

Frankfurt, Germany

Dear John,

I thank you very much for your long letter and for your invitation to take part in the reunion in Gloucester. I appreciate this invitation but due of my disability I cannot follow up your invitation. I fear I might not be able to stand the long journey and the strain and excitement of the reunion. I am 77! I would like to send you this letter and I want to tell you the story of your rescue as far as I can remember. Of course I have forgotten details but I think my report will be of interest for you and the other survivors. Our action wasn't heroic! It was a matter of course for me as a sailor to save other sailors without regard to their nationality! I am very glad that you are a sailor I could save and take on board of my sailing vessel!

This is a shortened story of the rescue of 80 survivors of the Gloucester.

In 1941 I was an officer in our air force. Because I had the master examination of the merchant navy I was ordered in April 1941 to join the rescue team in Greece. After a long time of looking for suitable boats to go to sea I found in Athens the very old sailing Greek Yacht "Omonia" and a motor boat belonging to the customs which was no longer there. My task was to be at sea in the north of Crete to save crews of our airplanes in case of emergency landing at sea during the fight in Crete. On the 20th of May we anchored with these boats in a bay of the small island "Antikythera". Next day we saw just before noon from a hill on this island on the horizon 11 big English warships sailing from the NE into the straights of Kythera. All the ships sailed in a keel-line with high speed and were shooting all their guns from all sides of the ships. They were attacked by our airforce planes by bombs and torpedoes. Suddenly we saw a huge cloud of dark smoke rising from one of your ships, it was the "Gloucester", illuminated by flames which soon covered the whole horizon. One of the following ships stopped to save the crew members of your sinking ship. But she was badly attacked by our airplanes and forced to give up the rescue operation following the other ships. As soon as the fleet was out of sight I ordered to lift anchor to look for survivors of this catastrophy. Because I had no exact position where the "Gloucester" had sunk and the helping-engine of my boat had broken down I could not reach the place until the next day after having searched for it the whole night in vain. The sea had become very rough and when I arrived at the place we saw among a lot of wreckage some gum boots with some people sitting in water which had filled their boats. The men were exhausted and could not catch hold the ropes we threw to them. We were forced to manoeuvre to each boat. The motor boat could have reached the place earlier and could have saved some more survivors. We also could save some men swimming with life belts in the rough sea. The following night it had become very stormy and it took a great effort for me to keep the "Omonia" without engine and by some storm-sails floating on the high sea. All my crew members had become sea-sick with the exception of me and another sailor. The next morning the sea was calmer and I could bring you to the east-coast of Greece. I think it was "Monemvasia".

This is the story of the rescue action as far as I can remember. Excuse my mistakes! My wife and I live alone now. All our four children are married and have their homes in other towns being not too far away from here.

I should like to close my letter. I think it's time to send it to you. I am sure you have much work to do in preparing the reunion in Gloucester.

Hoping you and your family are well and to get an answer from you I am with all best wishes.

Yours sincerely

Erich Wegner

The 'Fighting G Club' held their 50th Reunion on Wednesday May 22nd 1991. The few remaining survivors remembering the 723 shipmates that were lost. A special service was held in Gloucester Cathedral and wreaths were laid in memory. Erich had been invited to the ceremony and to the reunion, but had to decline. He had been seriously wounded in the leg (a week before the war finished) near Berlin. Prior to this he was firstly in the Navy, then attached to the Air Force and lastly transferred to the Army. At the time of the rescue Erich was a navigational officer, he rescued the 84 survivors and landed all on the island of Kythera. Total ship's company was 807, 723 lives sadly perished at the time. During my correspondence with Erich he had told me of a Guernsey- man named William Morellic who also was a survivor of the ship. His widow Mary has recently told me she also keeps in touch with the 'Fighting G Club' and with the reunions, as her husband William had been in the Navy for 37½ years. She had also met Erich and his wife Inge whilst they were on holiday in Guernsey.

THE FIGHTING "G" CLUB

President
Mr. J. Stevens
20 Barle Gardens,
South Ockendon,
Essex. RM15 5QP
Tel. (0708) 853388

Secretary
Mr. O. Gardiner
3 Chestnut Avenue,
Horndean,
Hants. PO8 9EU
Tel. (0705) 591345

H.M.S. GLOUCESTER 1939-41

Mr. John Stevens a survivor and the President of the 'Fighting G Club' has written to me this week — 1992. He writes of the 'Gallant Crew' and the sad loss of his mates — the honour to have 'met' up with Erich again and the respect he feels for him.

John writes — I'm very pleased you are to write about Erich. I have him to thank for my life as I was on my own, no life jacket, just hanging on to a beam of timber. But for him as Navigating Officer (although the enemy — as sailors we thought alike and had a spirit of comradeship about us), I would have perished. If it had not been for Erich as an Officer in the German Navy, I am certain the Paratrooper Officer on the Island of Kythera intended to shoot us all, he said this when we landed and I am sure he meant it, but for Erich's intervention.

Erich Wegner now in his eighties writes often (unless ill) telephones <u>every</u> Sunday morning and has done so for the past two or three years. How is your family? The weather? Enjoy your Sunday and keep well etc! Always the same talk but very sincere in his thoughts for us all.

He and his wife have invited André and I many times to their home in Frankfurt and when visiting other friends in Stuttgart this October we did make the effort to visit them for a day. We had a wonderful reception and were made most welcome. But now Erich suffers from Parkinsons Disease and could not fully enjoy our visit. Nevertheless we were very pleased and so was he to meet up again; the time taken up chatting to him just went by too quickly.

Now I feel with interest — the following letter is from an ex/German soldier who was amongst the Occupying forces on Guernsey and Sark. He wrote to me after being given my book by one of his friends in Germany.

18/08/89

Dear Mrs. Bihet,

I think you are looking forward to get some lines, as I promised to let you know all about my Guernsey stay. It started in 1943 after I became conscript and my unit was transferred from Eastern Europe to Guernsey. I do never forget this one lovely morning in September as we were disembarked at St. Peter Port Harbour.

Amazing this picturesque view up to the fascinating tiny houses around. The scenery seemed so peacefully, I couldn't believe in coming over here for purpose "to make war — to defend the island" as we were told. About the islands I couldn't imagine anything before. Officially they told us to come to Southern France — as maybe to keep for secret the real truth. After arrival at St. Malo we were embarked immediately at night I think for security reasons. My feelings told me out there I'm far away from the dangerous spots of this terrible war on the continent. These islands I was convinced were my luck and the chance of good to survive, or you say to overcome until the end of the war. The matter of fact for thinking in safeguard reasonably was the present of civilian population and thank goodness they are British! Never would be a struggle about the islands. And so it came out in the following as everybody knows. But please do let me continue. For some time we were stationed in a housing area, which seems to belong to St. Sampsons, uphill around a very nice little church beside a sports ground — could the Church be Annevilles Capelles? After a few months up there I was ordered to Castle Cornet. There I was picked out for a signal training based on a new light system. I had to be my job to get in contact to the Commanding Officer of the garrison headquarters in case of emergency — By the way I like to mention a special surprise which happened to me dear Mrs. Bihet as I came over for holiday reasons in 1975. I discovered my signal equipment in a glass cupboard as paying Castle Cornet a visit. By some people standing around I became a person of interest all of a sudden. They made photographs of me asking questions — and wanted to be informed about things in general at that time. (A little bit fuss about it, I didn't like it very much looking back). At this passage, please let me tell you where we used to stay during our two weeks holiday. There it has been the holiday accommodation of Mr. and Mrs. Lihau, 6 Sunrise Terrace, Rouge Rue, St. Peter Port. They were very nice people to us. Furthermore, it's worth mentioning a very kind Guernseyman we got acquainted to whom we were very grateful. Then it was a Mr. Cole, a grocer, whose shop he was running, was near the Gas Works. Alongside on the main road up to St. Sampson. I wonder if he's still there. We met each other very often and he used to show us around to the beautiful places.

But back to the 'bad days' you don't mind I continue. One day the silent days of Castle Cornet finished and I came up to the Isle of Sark. Everything seemed much different to the much loved Guernsey Island I got used to, even it was so smaller. Advantages to me the little practice of my french, as the spoken Patois seemed similar.

At that time, as you have to know, we were guarded over well by British Battleships around the clock, because the invasion had begun successfully in France in the meantime. Remembering the worst thing has been the shortage of food for nearly 12 months and nevertheless the complete cut off concerning the exchange of news from home. Because of the food I have had very good relationship to some Sark people as to be lucky in getting some food from time to time. In that state of a so called time of nerves we already discussed to get away plan to British ships at night. But those dangerous thoughts used to be rejected as one day a British bearer of a flag of truce sailed set to Guernsey. I've seen myself the peculiar boat and the big white flag. It was told they wanted to negotiate the withdrawal of all of us to Portugal or Spain. But regrettably nothing like that turned out, what a great pity. In all the time of the awaiting end draw nearer. Finally, the 8th May '45; the day of surrender in Germany, the V-Day came true. We now out here were looking forward for the British troops to come — Don't mind please I'm telling you another small story. (No) On the *same day I had to fulfil an extraordinary duty for to be a special envoy belonging to the administration staff so I was nominated to deliver a message to 'The Dame of Sark' Mrs. Sybil Hathaway from the Captain in Command — I may have some ideas concerning the content of the writing — so you can imagine? I was cycling down the decorated and well dressed up lanes everywhere and alongside them there were cheering people standing around — up to the residence. I do confess the anxious feelings in me, unable to predict the reaction of the Sarkees because of my German uniform, still wearing. The only thing was to speed up to come right through. But fill with amazement all of the crowd were waving happily at me and I did, waving back proudly the whole way.*

The war was over but nobody cared about us. No-one of a British soldier was ever seen. They have forgotten us, completely we said — as we were the smallest 'army' of 150 men left — a fortnight later, a small task force came over to take us gently in captivity finally. They hardly have had any work to do as we ourselves had sorted out our own weapons and equipment before in a usual correct German manner. Up on a British ship we sailed to Guernsey again, helping to clean up the island (for 12 months). I can't say the place where the camp supposed to be — maybe near Saumarez Park, wasn't it? I left Guernsey for Devonshire in '46. Another five years came by. Thankful for a British Colonel who took me out for Cultural activities. I have had a very good time indeed.

Dear Mrs. Bihet, this is the close my Guernsey story. I hope it was of some interest to you. Please don't mind some faults. Please remember me to your relations.

I may like to keep in contact to you.

Yours faithfully,

Werner Hostmann
Dreieich/Hessen
(Recently retired head school teacher)

July 14th 1989

August 15th 1989

Quite a number of Dutch people also holiday in the Island and they tell of tragedies and shortages. It appears (like in Guernsey) that folk living in the country fared much better than those living in the towns. One

Dutch lady kindly wrote and sent me the very touching sequel to the 'Anne Frank Story'. I had already read her first diary which was so tragic for a young girl.

Another lady who I had met in the market (I chat far more than I sell!), sent me her true story of when she was serving in the Wrens during the war. Another Mollie! 'Our Brethen Shield in Danger's Hour' by Mollie Crisford.

Also Renate Greenshields has written and sent her story as a child living in Germany during the war — 'Lucky Girl Goodbye'. All interesting reading.

Maybe it isn't such a bad thing to talk so much at the 'Olde Market' as I am accused of doing!

I think its that teasing devil John around again!

Through a conversation with a visitor 'Sue Fryer' of Rookery Farm, Oxfordshire whom I had never met before, kindly offered to type this book for me! I was explaining during the afternoon that a 'sequel' was in the making, but that our elder daughter Sally was finding it difficult to find the time (although a good typist) to help. She was working part-time but having to take the grandchildren here and there after school, her time was taken up with being a busy housewife too. Sue came back purposely to see me during the evening and offered her services! What a lovely gesture but I do hope she hasn't had any regrets! For me I have found another kind friend with excellent skills I have appreciated very much. Thanks Sue, we shall be keeping in touch.

CHAPTER 14

ALL ON RECORD

With receiving letters and odd parcels, I always feel sorry for people who receive very little, maybe this thought does stem back during those five years when very little mail was received and no magazines, national papers, comics, etc. A short letter can mean so much and especially so these days when everyone seems so busy. Two years ago a large package arrived for me which I felt was probably advertising matter and I put it aside until I had more free time to take a look. Leaving it until the evening, I had been totally mistaken and realised there were maybe a dozen or so large foolscap sheets of paper. I had never seen 'Braille' writing before and was most surprised to find these letters had been sent by scholars from the Royal National Institute for the Blind at the 'New College' Worcester. It was most touching for me and I can tell you I had a good cry thinking of these children who had bothered to write. They were asking all manner of questions stemming from my books and wanting me to answer regarding the family, especially of grandpa! (and my mother too). Of course the teachers had translated these letters for me, so it was only left for me to get cracking and answer back to all individually. They have (through their teacher) kept in touch with me since and through her I have known what grand work is done at the college and the progress of the children who have written.

Apparently the 'Director of Music' at the college (also blind), was living in Guernsey during the Occupation.

Before finishing let me say, I haven't forgotten you — Henry, Rachel, Philip, Sharon, Alice, Auriel, Maelea, Toby, Kevin, Julia — nor any of the children I have spoken to at the market. Emma, Kirsty and others — my love to you all.

Thankfully children nowadays have a totally different life to the days of my childhood.

But saying that, two very plucky U.K. Ranger Guides from Surrey wanted the 'delight' of sleeping in a German Bunker on the Island, and they did!! Apparently through reading my book they were inspired to find out more about the Occupation. The Guides camped at Les Mainguy Guide Headquarters and visited several former German installations.

By sleeping in the bunker, they used this as part of their study for the expedition section of the Queen's Guide Award. It was unfortunate I was away at this time, I never met Georgina Smith and the Rangers, but was pleased although most surprised to know of their 'episode' through reading my book.

TV recordings have been made — André and I were very fortunate in meeting the very pleasant BBC crew when making a South West programme — again of Occupation years and especially of Liberation time. Chris Slade of Spotlight SW interviewed me in our garden and Jill Dando (the BBC TV presenter) also enjoying a cup of tea and a relaxing hour after the interview, before they left on their busy schedule on the island. All the 'crew' were really nice, especially so the producer — Mr. Phil Jones of Plymouth with whom we still keep in touch.

I was also very fortunate with Irene to be chosen to join a small Guernsey party and travel to Birmingham and meet Roy Hudd the famous and very funny comedian to make a programme for Central TV. Roy put us immediately at ease for the 'Home Town' programme and we all had a wonderful time there.

For the past three years, there has been on sale a video 'Channel Islands Occupied' — produced by Brian Matthews. Brian had for many years loved Guernsey and had always wanted to produce a video of the occupation years. He felt so strong about it in the end, he had to actually mortgage his property to start with the necessary funds. Pleased to say he has now sold over 9,000 copies and the States of Guernsey has made it the 'Official Liberation Video'. A great success and my Guernsey colleagues gave an excellent account. I am afraid I am not a good speaker (although I can talk a lot!) and never will be, but I seem to relate and be able to talk of these times better to schoolchildren which I have been asked to do several times. It can be a little surprising when children ask questions though. The last school I was at, the classroom of 9 and 10 year-olds were firing questions non stop and caused a pause from me when a boy's voice asked me "did you know of any Jerry Bags then?" It has seemed very much of late, many reporters from the National newspapers would like the answer to that one!

The BBC recording team again came to Guernsey to film the 'Landmarks' for schools and shared an interesting programme mainly concentrating on the Fiftieth Anniversary of the evacuation of the Island's schools.

112

Previously a musical production was put on and acted with adults and 400 schoolchildren. 'A la Perchoine' meaning 'Till we meet again' or 'Till the next time'. It was greatly enjoyed by the Islanders but also being remembered by many with mixed feelings and with lumps in their throats I am sure.

A very good TV programme which included parts of 'A la Perchoine' was again repeated by the BBC.

'The Time, the Place' was another television programme I was involved in. Martin Le Page and I took part in the live programme, screened in Jersey in a bunker and also included tales from our Jersey colleagues. In 1985, soon after the printing of my book, Radio Guernsey recorded a series of 'In the Old School Yard' and memories of the Occupation years were featured which Islanders find most interesting. More recently, Mr. Conrad Wood came to Guernsey and made lengthy recordings to be made available at the Imperial War Museum. Over recent years he has already interviewed some well known personalities from these years and who sadly are no longer with us; so it is very gratifying to know the true accounts of the Channel Island's war has been well and truly recorded for future generations and will be available amongst the history sections in libraries, museums and archives.

CHAPTER 15

A MURDER IN LES CANICHERS! GUERNSEY'S LAST HANGING

The meaning of Les Canichers (which is in four parts as we have a lower, main, back or upper and narrow Canichers!) could have come from the French word 'La Corniche' meaning a little path at the base of a Cliff. Another meaning of 'Canichers' I've seen described as being 'hidden' or 'hiding places' but to André and I. Les Canichers, St. Peter Port is a nice, 'comfortable', warm and friendly road with many old 'character' houses. Most haven't changed names over the years. One has always been called 'Psycho', and for a long while has had a garden full of different figures — animals, birds, mermaids, etc, but mostly gnomes which Michael who lives there has mostly made out of plaster of paris moulds. There's fisherman gnomes, gardening gnomes and playful gnomes, all sorts — all brightly painted with smiling faces and Les Canichers just wouldn't be the same without them. Michael tells me he belongs to a group on the mainland called the 'Society for the Prevention of Cruelty to Garden Gnomes!' At least the ones in his garden look very happy and contented, even the ones perched on the garage roof and on the gutters of the tall house!! Michael's Mother — Mrs. Winnie Green was living at 'Psycho' at the time of Occupation and worked as a waitress at the Royal Hotel. The chef would greet her with 'Good Morning Mrs. Green, Heil Hitler' — although not German, she was Swiss and very pro German. It was unfortunate for Mrs. Green as when she replied with 'Good Morning Chef, Heil Churchill', she was arrested for insulting the Fuhrer. She was tried and sentenced to six months in prison. We all knew Mrs. Green (Winnie) very well and was most shocked to know she had to go away to serve her sentence. After the six months, she returned from a Caen jail in France.

But a very much more serious offence occurred during the latter part of the year 1853. During that time I am sure, Les Canichers would not have been nice and comfortable. A murder was committed! This episode was stated as being 'an event which excited a painful interest

114

in our Guernsey community'. During the evening of October 18th, a 74 year old lady, Elizabeth Saujon, had spent an evening with lady friends enjoying tea and talking of her lodgers who helped out her meagre income. She was a widow, her late husband André being a Frenchman and a former soldier of France. He had been a good husband and had worked in Guernsey as a storeman — both being very respected in the community. She continued to live in her home at 'Les Canichers' after André's death and had been living there for 40 years. Nothing unusual about the day or evening and she was in good spirits when she said 'goodnight' to her friends at 9 p.m.

But next day, her neighbour noticed Mrs. Saujon's shutters were still closed — he knocked at the door but got no answer. He rushed to another house in the Canichers where a 'High Constable' lived and was joined by a passer-by and another neighbour, a carpenter. All four men were concerned and climbed through an upstairs window by ladder, then went downstairs into the sitting room. They were met with suffocating smoke and when entering Mrs. Saujon's bedroom, staggered back with horror with what they smelt and had found. She was dressed in her usual manner, but it was obvious she was horribly dead. Parts of her body were burnt to a cinder, other parts slightly scorched. The room was smouldering with the heat and only because the doors and windows were tightly closed, cutting out essential air, had stopped the whole room bursting into flames.

The bedrooms had been ransacked and a neighbour pointed out many articles of value were missing — neither could money be found. Paraffin had been splashed all over the room.

The dignatories of the Island, the Bailiff and Jurats, the Queen's Procurer Substitute and the Police all visited the house of death. After an autopsy, doctors found that Mrs. Saujon had suffered a serious head wound and that burning must have started before life was extinct. The old lady of a pleasant disposition had died in acute agony, she had been toasted alive.

One can only imagine how the residents of the road (where most of the houses are joined and close together), must have felt and been appalled by the tragedy. The whole Island too. My great grandfather must have also taken a special interest, as at the time he was living at 'Rose Villa' number 30. He was 21 years of age and was either a lawyer at the time, or studying to be one.

After enquiring at neighbours, the Police learned of a man called Simmer who had lodged with Mrs. Saujon for a few months, accompanied by a woman he said was his wife. He had been seen walking up and down near the house, between 9 and 10 p.m. on the night of the murder. Mrs. Saujon had told friends that Simmer had been bargaining with her about a table he wanted to buy. They couldn't agree about the price — the widow wanted £2 but he offered less — final agreement being 35/-.

Simmer was traced to be living at Les Hubits, St. Martin's — and although known as Simmer in St. Peter Port, was known as John Charles Tapner in St. Martins. He was 30 years of age and working in the Engineer's Department at Fort George. From an honest family and of a religious father, he was born in Woolwich and had been well educated.

Tapner denied being anywhere near the house (not sure which one) in the Canichers but witnesses distinctly remembered seeing him wearing a glazed hat and monkey jacket and carrying a heavy stick at the crucial time.

Tapner was also up to his eyes in debt. He had to support his wife Mary and three children in St. Martin's. He also kept Margaret (his wife's sister) and their newborn baby in lodgings at the Vale Road. Mary had no idea her sister was even in the Island, let alone keeping company with Tapner. He drank heavily and earned only £120 per year.

Suddenly after the murder it was noted he began to pay off his debts. When searching his rooms, hairs were to be found attached to items of his clothing, also a heavy bamboo walking stick. Police kept watch at midnight and after visiting a field opposite the house, found in a haystack many of the missing items from the Canichers house. This was enough for Tapner to be arrested. He appeared in the Royal Court on October 28th charged with murder and theft of many valuable items, plus £30 in Guernsey notes (which was certainly a lot of money in 1853).

Special arrangements were made to accommodate the big crowds to hear the evidence of 70 witnesses. Tapner protested his innocence, but the Bailiff and the 12 Jurats of the Royal Court after 12 full days listening to all the evidence was found guilty, and sentenced to death by hanging.

Victor Hugo, the French writer then living in exile in Jersey was a great fighter against capital punishment and he decided to take up the case. He together with Tapner appealed to the Lord Palmerston and Queen Victoria to spare his life but they both said 'no' — the law must take its course. Apparently whilst at the town prison, he and his wife Mary were reconciled and two days before his execution, he finally admitted his guilt to four reverend gentlemen who visited him.

Apparently, 25 years previous to this, a French emigrant named Beasse, had publicly swung from the gallows on a St. Peter Port beach after having to walk through hissing crowds in the High Street and along the Esplanade with the rope around his neck.

116

JOHN CHARLES TAPNER,
AS HE WAS SEEN   THE NIGHT HE COM-
MITTED THE BARBAROUS MURDER OF
MRS. E SAUJON.

Executed February 10, 1854.

Now Victor Hugo made valiant efforts to avoid a similar situation and with the Guernsey authorities being ashamed, decided the hanging would be around St. James Church and the Elizabeth College. Scaffolding was built and a trap door beneath. But with the trap door too narrow, Tapner was able to hang on by his elbows to the edges, wedging himself for some 15 minutes whilst two men grabbed his legs from below and hung on until he finally had to let go and was strangled to death. It took 15 minutes for Tapner to die and 'the execution was a dreadful thing' wrote Hugo. In a letter of protest to Lord Palmerston. Victor Hugo discloses that the hanging was botched — the Executioner had never built a scaffold before and had made the trapdoor far too narrow.

A superstition at this time brought many people for a cure of epilepsy. Those suffering arrived and touched the cold and stiff hand of Tapner and even placed his hands over their faces.

The superstition was believed to be a certain cure with a touch of a hanged man. Souvenir hunters also rushed for bits of the rope — even after the rope was burnt, the hunters raked the ashes for mementoes!

Victor Hugo paid three francs for Tapner's death mask which had been made still bearing the marks of the rope and distended veins of the neck. Tapner lies buried in Upland Road cemetery, St. Peter Port, alongside the other Guernsey murderer, the exiled Frenchman Biasse. No man or woman has been hanged in Guernsey since the execution of John Charles Tapner on February 10th 1854.

I feel sure this terrible tragedy and murder of Elizabeth Saujon did not take place at 'Woodcote', nor at 'Rose Villa', the family home of Rose Villa number 30 had been in the Collins Family for many, many years long before this time and probably since it had been originally built.

CHAPTER 16

DONKEYS VERSUS CRAPAUDS!

As I am sure you are all aware, there is, and always has been, a friendly rivalry between the islands of Guernsey and Jersey. I can always remember the importance of Guernsey winning the football 'Murratti' and vice versa when attending the 'Track' many years ago. Like hundreds of others, we would support our team and when Jersey played football on their own ground, many including 'Gramp' would go down for the day.

Like many other young men from Guernsey, gramp and dad in their very early teens and as young men would work long hours in Jersey collecting and picking up potatoes during the 'potato' season.

I'm sure these visits were the only time grandpa would have left the Island and the last time he travelled with the 'lads' was when he was aged 89! He was very proud of his popular grandson Les Collins as he really was the star of the team and at one time was offered the chance to join the professional 'Arsenal' team but I believe, loved Guernsey and home too much to leave. André and I remember very well the time when Les and others of our age were playing and the young people who came up for the important football 'Cup Final' between the two islands (usually held April or early May),. There was much noise and clatter around the town after the boat trip came in! Usually the crowds brought with them, or they invaded the shops buying cheap saucepans and frying pans to clash together (the noisier the better) then rattles of all kinds and bells etc. Anything to be heard and seen (green and white for Guernsey — red and white for Jersey — and not forgetting Alderney, being blue and white)! I expect the same happened when in Jersey — Remember the chant? 1-2-3-4 who the hell are we for — G.U.E.R.N.S.E.Y. (then a shout altogether) GUERNSEY! or from the others — JERSEY! Along the Esplanade it was a continual din which we could hear from home. It was fun though, and all the young people found themselves at the 'Track' as you can judge for yourselves —

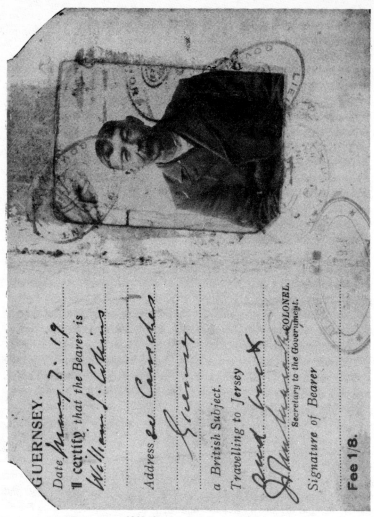

1919. Gramps permit to travel

most times the attendance was between six and eight thousand and sometimes more than that!

Alternate years when the Jersey team played Guernsey, we had an invasion of the 'Battrick Family', all well known Jersey fishermen (and sons), sometimes with wives, always came to mum and dad usually for lunch but would sometimes stay overnight. Naturally we had not seen any of the Jersey Battricks during the Occupation. So as a treat, my father suggested that mum, Joyce and I take a short air trip to see them soon after the liberation when flights re-started. We were excited but I believe a little nervous to go — we enjoyed the flight down and had a lovely day and saw the family, especially satisfied to see the mum and gran of all the Battricks (she was lovely). We set off for home.

Boarding the small aircraft, we were very soon ready for the short flight or so we thought! The pilot thought differently and gave us all a much longer flight and fright! He decided we were going to have an exciting trip but we were all terrified! He rocked, swayed, went right up and then swooped down, circled Herm very low three or four times and generally showed us what he could do. He almost looped the loop several times and we just sat there; separated too, everyone just held their breath. The other passengers spoke harshly to the pilot after landing and reported him to the authorities. We really did not hear any more but wondered if he was a war time pilot and wanted to show off his skills, or he might have been still celebrating our Liberation! We all remember this first flight and the treat dad gave us which could have ended in disaster quite easily.

Because dad was busy with so much repair work on the Island and employing more new workmen, dad had no free time at all but he wanted us to enjoy breaks, especially for mum's sake so he also treated mum, Joyce and I to a short holiday to friends in London when allowed after the war ended, we especially loved the train rides and the hundreds of pigeons at Trafalgar Square! What an eye-opener for us and great excitement, with no scares like our journey we had from Jersey.

With dad's business picking up I remember well the travelling salesmen visiting the Islands and coming home speaking to dad. A Mr. Austin from a firm in Bristol mentioned to dad he knew a young teenager who wanted a Guernsey penfriend — hence the start of a lovely friendship between Joan Davis (now Mrs. Dennis Hughes) and myself for over 47 years! Apart from a day's trip up from Jersey with her mother, we've yet to have a proper time together. We keep trying!

Although we are close to Jersey, it is not often we travel there, but last year after some 20 years gap, André and I spent three days there and we visited a son of one of the 'Battrick boys' from many years ago — Wally Battrick from St. Aubin boatyard. As soon as we met he recognised me from over 40 years ago and said his very fond memories of Guernsey all those years before was arriving on the Island with his teenage pals and just turning up at our home 'Rose Villa' before or after the 'Murratti'. He said no matter how many friends arrived with him, they were always made welcome and 'aunty Glad' always found somewhere to put them up for the night. He fondly spoke of mum and dad too as dad never minded the 'Invasion' — especially if Guernsey won and beat the 'crapauds'!

Mum and dad welcomed everyone into their home, No. 30 was an ever open door and a madhouse most times, many neighbours and friends used to pop in just for a laugh and chat and of course a cup of tea. One would have thought after liberation, she and dad would have wanted to just settle down with Joyce, myself and Gramp, seeing our uncles and cousin had now been rejoined with aunts, but no, friends had arrived back from England and had returned to find no home and no furniture. Being sorry for them, knowing these friends from many years before the War, mum and dad offered for the 'Mastertons' to live with us until they could get a home together.

The family were split up as did happen with many returning. Mr. Masterton (uncle Jim) stayed on in England for a while, Jean a daughter stayed with relations on the Island and Betty and her mum (aunty Edie) stayed several months and we enjoyed having them. Although I must say Betty has always thought of me as grannie and had a laugh about me coming up to bed with curlers in my hair and an old shawl! She still teases me now but I think she was dreaming! Honest!

Sunday morning walk with dad

CHAPTER 17

IT WAS MOTHER'S LIFE WITH A CONTENTED DAD

Dad as a younger man was a very good swimmer and a polo player. Being so tall he was able to stand on the sea bed most of the time, very handy as most times he was in goal! He then became the States diver having to look for and finding interesting items in and around the harbour; items lost from boats. André and I (at our age!) made a *first* visit to the very impressive and interesting Castle Cornet recently and I was reminded of dad's work being a diver those many years ago. Divers at this time were employed probably with very little pay and having to work in very heavy and clumsy gear. (Suits on display at the Castle). They saw to underwater damage to boats, they cleared fouled propellers and helped to raise sunken ships and saw to general work at the harbour (and still do of course). He loved this job and always said how fascinating underwater was, but had to retire as his ears were troubling him with bleeding after dives. He was first a footballer, then a referee — keen on all sports. When older, through his interests he and mum would attend and enjoy different functions. They loved the special 'Fancy Dress' dances, anything for a bit of fun. In every photograph taken of dad, he was making funny faces just to make people laugh. Although he was good looking and a fine man, it is most difficult to find a serious photograph of him amongst our big collection. I have also come across envelopes and postcards recently, dated late 40's and early 50's addressed to 'the mad Finigans' and to the 'Happy Finigans' – (I think these say it all!).

Of course dad could be serious and outside the Church at André's and my wedding, he was serious and was a little upset too. I just know, although he felt happy on our day, he was also a little sad too and my feelings were the same, a bit emotional. Saying that, he was soon his old self at the reception and dance at aunty Edie's and uncle Billy's tea room at 'Peary Nook', Vazon. It was their gift to us for the wedding and they certainly did us proud, with aunty Edie making and icing a

December 9th 1954

Mum and dad – even on a holiday in Switzerland! 1960's

lovely three tiered wedding cake. Very professional it was — she was an excellent cook.

Our wedding was on December 9th 1954 at St. Joseph's Church. We had booked to have a honeymoon in Jersey, but it was not to be. The weather was cold and blustery for our wedding and because of the gales, the 'mail boat' was over 20 hours late arriving in the Island from Weymouth! We decided to cancel so we spent our first night in our 'cold' unaired cottage, it was freezing cold, so I ended up wearing André's warm wincyette pyjamas! Very romantic.

In the following May, we travelled to Bournemouth for our delayed honeymoon and had no idea Sally was travelling with us!

Mum and dad were married also in December — the 27th, 1926 and also like us at St. Joseph's Catholic Church in St. Peter Port. They were married with a 'special' licence at 6.00 a.m. — a dark cold morning and dad always told everyone that he had been in the dark ever since! They managed to sail on the early morning boat to Jersey and stayed with my aunt and uncle Kath and Ted Finigan for a couple of days.

It was a couple years after their marriage that mum and dad were thrilled to know a baby was on the way. When the time was due and all was arranged for the midwife to attend, mum arrived at 'Rose Villa' (as was natural) wanting her mother to be present for the birth, but to everyone's surprise and especially to mum, she gave birth to twins! An

125

identical boy and girl — mum having one arrive without the midwife being present! It was wonderful news and everyone was thrilled, especially my father. Apparently he was so proud and excited, he wanted to tell everyone and was at every door in the neighbourhood with the news. The babies weighed over 4lbs. each and mum and dad have often said how beautiful they were, just like dolls. The babies were fed during their short life with fountain pen fillers but with no modern aid, nor intensive care, their lives were very short. Sadly for mum, dad and the family the excitement was short lived as they only lived for two or three days, after being christened William and Betty.

Because of this sadness and tragedy so early in their married lives, I'm sure mum and dad were quite 'soft' with Joyce and I. It's strange that besides the smiles one remembers in a 'close' person, I can picture so well my father's large 'hairy' and very dependable hands. The hands that had worked so hard for us and the same hands that had just tapped me once when I was a toddler for saying 'no' to him. I cried and howled so much and for so long in my bedroom, he had to fetch me down, give me a cuddle and he vowed then that he would never tap or hurt me again — which he didn't. After this and all through his life, I respected him and knew his look when he was not pleased with me.

He was a fine example to me and we were very close always. Not all the family felt like this towards dad though and a very favourite uncle of mine, Sid Collins, could willingly have bashed him many times I'm sure, though in fun! Mum's brother never did thank him for the life he gave him, he really teased the life out of him every time they were together, uncle Sid had no real answer to dad's teasing and it kept on for years — a shame really but underneath it all, uncle Sid loved it and him. They really thought a lot of each other and uncle Sid was as much upset as I at dad's funeral. Like us all, he missed dad an awful lot; and now with sadness we miss our dear uncle Sid, but pleased to say, our aunty Win his widow, is still well and able to remember with fondness the laughs at both their antics.

Mum's brother Sid and aunty Win (plus dad!)

Mum had always seemed to be caring for and nursing family and friends. The 'Angel' of the district, she was, always popping in to this one and that one, helping out wherever she could. Where help was needed, she was there and always done cheerfully, especially I remember her visiting (occasionally I went with her) a house in Bosq Lane twice a day making an old gentlemen confined to bed comfortable and this went on for many months (even years). He had just wanted to stay in his own home until the end and it was mother who found that he had passed away. Mum was always on call to everyone, folks would say 'Get our Glad, she'll come' — and always she would drop everything to do what she could when anyone was in trouble. Even to 'laying' out those who had passed on — she took charge and gave much support to those around her. I had also

Fun at the old party games

mentioned in 'A Child's War' she had found an elderly neighbour, Cliff Holloway in the house in the 'Back Canichers'. Mum found him with his head in the gas oven. She had helped him throughout the five years Occupation, his only son being killed in action at the beginning of the War, his wife having evacuated, she returned, and suddenly died soon after her return. Being depressed and saddened, he had committed suicide; suddenly Mr. Holloway had nothing to live for, or to look forward to.

Mum also had great worry and concern for her sister, who lived in the next road, Paris Street, who suffered greatly at time with mental breakdowns. This sickness really began during the Occupation when her gas ration for cooking (and some lighting) ran out. Mother could see the signs and helped all she could, but aunty Al finally just had to be taken to the hospital. She was a big lady and at these times, difficult to handle. It was unfortunate too for mum and the family that these spells happened time and time again. I have always thought remembering my aunt (and mother too), that a physical sickness is much easier to cope with than a mental one. Mum had nursed her mother from a stroke until she died, helped to nurse my other gran and looked after a great aunt nursing her with cancer until the end. Grandpa was luckily only in bed for the last fortnight, but he also died at home — she took everything in her stride and got on with what she had to do.

I happened to visit an old friend of mum's and her daughter (who used to nurse at the 'Town Hospital' years ago) was also there at the time. The ex-nurse said she could never forget mum and her regular visits to the Old People's Hospital in Hospital Lane (now the new Island Police Station). Usually three or four times a week with small goodies for all, and cuddles and kisses for everyone. Despite not being too clean or 'fresh' at the time (nurses remark!), she had time and love and smiles for everyone, no matter who they were and whether she knew them or not. Only very recently I have made friends with a lady who asked me last week what my maiden name had been. On saying 'Finigan' she immediately mentioned 'Gladys — I thought so' — Then she went on to tell me of mothers antics and the many laughs she caused whilst a patient in hospital during the Occupation — then at the Emergency Hospital. Tessa, a nurse then, said she and the other nurses had never laughed so much in all their lives and had never forgotten her for this. What a tonic for everyone around her at such a time!

Whilst in business, dad came home one day and told mum he had been to an auction and bought a house for them to move into. He thought she would be happy there as it was far more convenient than 'Rose Villa' and situated not too far away, 'The Moorings' was on the seafront, on the Esplanade and had wonderful sea views. But no! Mum did not even want to take a look. She was determined to stay and like 'Pop' of old, was not going to move house for anyone, even though by what Dad had said, it was far nicer than any house he'd ever seen and for him and his finances, he could just about manage to buy it. He was so thrilled about it, but realised it was no good — mum had made up her mind despite his good intention. He knew the previous bidder, so telephoned that evening and offered to sell it to him should he still be interested. Yes he was, he bought it from dad for the same price, but I believe dad gained a small patch of land through the deal. There were no regrets on dad's part and he stayed contented at No. 30 until the end of his days.

THE BARREL ORGAN PLAYED AND PLAYED!

Mum had worked very hard for over 40 years for the 'British Legion' and continued to do so until she was past 80 years of age. At the top of the Arcade Steps near the Market Square, many will remember ma and the music and the reputation of the old barrel organ played all day long to raise money for the 'Poppy Appeal Fund.' She often found friends and visitors who would also take a turn at turning the handle and usually another Legion Member, Mr. Roland, would have joined to help her. In latter years, because the organ needed attention, she was

Mum and dad enjoying the garden at Rose-Villa

always given a chair in 'Boots' doorway, and many of the locals always saved (and sent) their donation to 'Glad' or 'aunty Glad'. She had been collecting money for many years and had raised a considerable amount for the Legion, but also for the 'Battle of Britain — The Royal Air Force'. She was thought of very highly by Major John Willis, Chairman of the Poppy Appeal organisation and also by her many friends with whom she worked preparing the poppies before the day. One member Mr. Le Cornu has always spoken of her as the salt of the earth — 'one of the best.' There was always a lot of preparation to do and deliveries to be made, but she always felt it was for a very good cause having seen her brother Reg die through wounds received during the First World War.

He had a bullet lodged in his spine for some 26 or 27 years! After the operation to remove the bullet, gangrene set in. Not having the suitable drugs on the Island at the time during the Occupation, he had died in 1942. Another of mum's brothers 'Bill' who had for many years a shoe shop in the Pollet (where mum had also worked before her marriage), had lost an arm in the First World War. She never forgot their friends and the many sad cases she had known of at Roehampton Hospital, therefore she always wanted to play her part. During her membership, she wore her uniform very proudly, marching as an escort to the 'flag' and was still selling poppies when she was 80 years old

*Mr Roland and mum raising money for the 'Battle of Britain'
with the barrel organ*

*Collecting with another friend, Hilda le Cras
who still works hard for the 'Poppy' fund*

from 8.00 a.m. till late and most times in cold, windy and damp weather.

Mum as an escort on parade

Mum also enjoyed very much her weekly game of bowls and her other great love for many years was playing cards, 'whist' and 'euchre' — any game really she enjoyed. Gradually, over the years, her eyesight was getting worse as she suffered with glaucoma and cataracts. Her poor eyesight finally took hold and she had to resign to the fact she couldn't play with her friends at 'Drives' any more. I well remember one gent who visited and stayed with us for many years and who also would visit the local whist drives whilst on holiday. I would usually take him and mum by car, but if busy he and mum would take a taxi and go together. Mum used to get much teasing about him by other guests at home but she'd also enjoy the laugh about her 'boyfriend' for the fortnight. André and I understood him and liked him very much but he was a most unhappy elderly bachelor who lived alone. He had never made friends easily at 'Woodcote' and neither did he at the Whist Drives! He was a very keen player but when someone played the wrong card he showed his annoyance very much and upset the other 'whisters' — mum's friends. They were all very pleased when our 'Pop Jennings's' fortnight was up but strangely, André never watches the Cup Final in May without mentioning Pop and remembering his company then. Mum got on with 'Pop' also, and with everybody. Especially with these close friends of hers and none better than Mrs. Phyllis Cox who would collect her and bring her home after the drives, others too, always willing to give a lift. Most Saturdays 'our Phyl' would collect ma and take her for a ride in the country and around the coast, then they'd enjoy a bar meal together. Phyl really was a very dear friend of mum's, just like dear Edie Wilcox was earlier, not only to mum but to us and to many others also. Too few of these lovely characters around us; these were three of a 'special' kind.

Not only did mum love the old people, children too, and years ago always seemed to have younger children around at home. I remember every year mum (with dad sometimes), going into the town before Christmas, and after finding out children's ages etc., would choose lovely gifts for each and every child at Guernsey's Children's Homes. The shops would deliver an extra gift from 'Father Christmas' and the children would be very grateful at both Homes for mum and dad's gifts. Also they'd have a lot of pleasure visiting at the time.

Good 'old Glad' or 'Gladys' as everyone called her always loved the town and would usually take a walk and do some shopping every morning — always her cheery remark 'Hello my love' — and everyone knew mum. Her temperament was always the same, placid and a smile and a wave for all. The town was always busy then, and one met everyone there, it was impossible to get far without 'chatting' — constantly.

Mum was a very generous lady and loved giving — to young and elderly, those usually she met in the town less fortunate than herself. Talking of giving, there was a funny incident one day just after we were liberated when mum was chatting in Woolworths with an old friend and 'Canichers' neighbour who had just returned from the mainland. 'Aunty Gert' to Joyce and I but always referred affectionately as 'skinny Gert' by mum and dad. Whilst chatting, a lady approached them and gave aunty Gert a £1 note to treat herself to some chocolates 'you deserve it' she said 'I can see you've had a very lean time over here!' Mum must have looked quite healthy and fit alongside her old friend as Gert was so terribly thin. Neither knew this generous lady but all together shared a laugh, can't remember what happened to the £1 note!

We have always had nice neighbours as good friends nearby especially Mrs. Jane (Harriet) and granny Hamon who live next door to Rose Villa and opposite 'Woodcote'. Mum would pop in and have a chat with Jane and her 98 year old mother — a wonderful old lady with a memory to match and it was always a pleasure seeing them all together enjoying a laugh. These two 'Harriets' widows of the same names (Hamons) are 'Sarkees'. Hamon is a typical Sark surname like 'Carre', 'de Carteret' and 'Perree'. When mum reached 80 years of age amongst our past neighbours were the very nice Sue, Jeff and Simon Le Cras who lived next door. On mum's birthday we had such a surprise as they had climbed up from their garden and we found a massive banner that stretched right across 12' of our balcony at the rear of our house. It was certainly a surprise to us and to mum. Sue and Jeff had crept early morning and placed it there, having taken a lot of time and trouble to make this huge colourful 'Rainbow' with large lettering 'HAPPY 80th BIRTHDAY GLADYS, THE WHOLE STREET LOVES YOU' and, she dearly loved the street!

Outing with friends 1990. Phyllis Cox (left) with mum (right) and Cliff Falla in background (see later).

CHAPTER 18

ENTER THE DINOSAURS!

When mum and dad did go dancing mum hated sitting it out. She had loved dancing all her life and as a younger woman was apparently well sought after to dance with being light on her feet and full of life. Many admirers I'm sure, as she was a very attractive young lady but dad was the only one she cared for or looked at. They had been together since being 13 or 14 years of age. The old 'Pillar Hall' was the 'in' place for young people in the 20s and 30s, the 'Charleston Days'. When mum and dad got married, they were presented with a very fine silver tea set from their friends at the 'Pillar Hall'.

For André and my age group the 'in' place was St. George's Hall on the Esplanade. A rather basic hall but with a wonderful large dance floor with lots of atmosphere and a good sound from the 'The Georgians'. I remember also wanting to make the most of Saturday evenings by dancing all the time. Now its tap dancing around the kitchen table! When feeling fit I still go to classes and up to a few months ago I was one of the 'Guernsey Roly Polys'!

It was some six years ago that five nurses from the King Edward Hospital decided to form a 'Dancing' group to get together a show for the patients at Christmas. Having two dressmakers in the group, attractive costumes were made and because of the size of the ladies concerned and the costumes at the time, green, a name was chosen — 'DOTTIE' (THE LITTLE ONE) AND THE DINOSAURS. They were a great success, a good laugh and after one lady had to drop out, I was asked whether I would like to join. Being rather large and a bit silly like the others. I seemed to fit in alright. Mind you, it did not stop at hospital shows, we were asked to join variety shows for charity raising. More rehearsing had to be done and all credit to May Ogier who had the patience and time to try and make something out of us 'amateurs'.

We were kindly offered a Dance Studio to practise in but after a while unfortunately had to resort to May's garage cum greenhouse. It was great fun though and everyone seemed to enjoy our prancing about

Molly, Ann Hards, Maggie Mauger, May Ogier, Little Dottie Martin.

and miming of songs. It was our shapes that caused the laughs, Dottie putting us to shame by her small frame of seven stone! All together our ages totalled 268 years and combined weight was 68 stones! You can imagine the yardage needed for several different costumes! The ideas and styles of these outfits were a credit to Anne and May, and they, the costumes if nothing else always caused a stir! We helped raise an awful lot of money and danced many times at different hotels, mainly the 'Wayside Cheer' where the Sunday evening shows were a great success. We danced at several schoolrooms, Church halls, anywhere when we could and were asked, especially around Christmas time to dance for the handicapped, the children and the elderly.

We even appeared as five 'dainty' nymphs in a Church Pantomime! Can you imagine! I caused a lot of laughter one evening when going on stage and imagining just how we 'fairies' looked like. I couldn't stop laughing thinking how silly we were — then the audience joined in the laughing too. This also caused the cast to forget their lines for a couple of minutes and laughter from them too — everyone was in fits. That wasn't the end as the next evening during the performance, Maggie decided to wear oversized wellington boots with her dainty frilly costume and came in staggering around!

Enough said! Last year sadly and 'gracefully' 'Dotty and the Dinosaurs' finished. I really think May's husband Harry 'our manager and friend' had also put up with his 'Girls! Girls! Girls!' long enough!

My other hobby during the past five or six years has been swimming, trying to keep up with the 'wet friends' all year round. It has not been successful as far as I am concerned! I am no great swimmer but I do enjoy the feeling of the sea. During winter and springtime, one cannot stay swimming in the temperatures around our shores for long, but a small group of 'wet' people, manage a dip every day of the year.

Some of the hardier ones stay in a good while, while others will have a 'tea bag' dip. It was a lovely October morning when I decided to take a walk down to La Vallette pools and have a coffee — seeing familiar faces as one always does on a small island such as ours — I joined the group and had a chat. Of course it led to 'aren't you coming in?'. It was lovely and I enjoyed their company. On leaving, it was 'see you tomorrow!' (remark from Jean as always). So when I could manage to go these past few years, it has given me great pleasure just knowing and having such lovely friends; even though I'm not usually 'wet'. I must confess to making some poor excuses for not going in! I know the younger 82 years olds (like Bill Green who loves my Bean Jar!) and the young 70 plus's like Alf Le Poidevin and Bernie Amy, Marion Jouhning, etc. etc., the Mad Nobby Norman will forgive me if I just mention Stella Hunt in particular as she is aged 92 and a regular all year round swimmer. The only time when she doesn't is when the tide is very high and thrashing on the rocks. We all admire her very much and she is an inspiration to us all, one can hardly believe she has reached 92 years looking and keeping so active like she does. The sea can be very dangerous to anyone, unless a very powerful swimmer, but many or most still do swim — even in snow. (Fortunately Guernsey has very little, but the cold north-east winds can be biting at times.)

It really has been a pleasure knowing each and every one, they come from all parts of the Island and from different walks of life. The main aim is to simply take everyone as they are, have a laugh and just enjoy the company of each other. I have felt very privileged to be part of the group and sincerely hope to remain so for many future years. (Many visitors join us year after year, you'd be made welcome too! 10.30 a.m.!)

It was these friends and others who helped make my 60th birthday a special one recently. Do you know up until 1991, André in all his 63 years, had never set foot on Sark? Not for the want of my trying, but for Liberation Day the C.I. Occupation Society organised a day there with the visiting Liberation 135 Task Force as a varied programme is always made for their visit. André thoroughly enjoyed the day and made the suggestion to have another trip for my birthday. I was pleased, but surprised after all these years, he'd want to make a second visit in the same year. Arrangements were made, we'd have a family barbecue at Sally's when we came back. André and I were both tired after tramping around Sark and as we struggled up Bosq Lane I said I

With Sally, Michael and the grandchildren
'Woodcote' August 1991

was just about ready for bed! Oh but no, I spotted Carol with a video hiding opposite the house and when reaching home, it dawned on me why I was sent off for the day. I have never seen so many balloons, flags, slogans, 'I am 60' ribbons etc. etc. all across the railings and windows. Everyone had been in no doubt. Inside was the same, but also plates and plates of goodies, all sorts, drinks etc. You name it, everything had been got ready for a surprise party. Sally, Carole and André of course had arranged this and the girls had been busy all day. I had no idea who would be coming, so it was a pleasant surprise to see some old friends again. Next morning I took the remaining food and drink down to the pools to finish the celebrations with my 'wet' friends. Ah! La Bonne Vie!

Those Dinosaurs again, 1989!

CHAPTER 19

WITH MUM A PARTICULAR WORRY

It is not surprising that our road 'Les Canichers' has, and always will mean alot to me. 'Rose Villa' too, but sadly it is not now in the family. Mother did expect that one day it would be sold as she had mentioned to Sally our elder daughter 'You can do whatever you like with Rose Villa after I've gone'. As Sally had got older and started a family she did enjoy and help me quite a lot serving guests' meals, so much so she and Michael were seriously thinking of starting a guest house too (when thinking of moving recently) but after making enquiries they realised the laws and regulations to start afresh would have been too costly. Rose Villa was also not convenient to alter so she continued to look at properties and kept her part-time job. They really wanted to move into the country, with more garden and the luxury of a garage! Since mum has passed away, Sally, Michael and children Ryan and Carly have now moved away towards Vazon (what a long way!) where they have settled happily in their new home. I am so pleased and grateful that mum never knew of the move and pleased to think that 'Rose Villa' is still a family home (not flats) and that it is being well cared for and loved.

Sally was pleased to be away from traffic that really does race through here and the very busy tea time hour. Thinking back there were never any problems when we were younger living here. When very young the road was always safe and clear to play ball, hop-scotch and I can remember as a teenager practising up and down on a very high old fashioned second-hand bicycle, and my very first bike! With all the traffic nowadays I really don't think I could get away with cycling now like I used to in my teens. Irene in the end gave up on me and refused to ride with me! I seemed to think all traffic would stop when I turned right, those cars in front and behind — all for me and there were times when I indicated to turn left but changed quickly to the right. I really had no road sense and for travelling out of the town area I was lost! Each time I visited her home at Pont Vaillont she would have to draw a little route map as to how I could get there. For the previous five years we had gone no-where and the Vale was a long way! (that's my excuse anyway) Times have changed and the pace of life has changed. I only wish my mother and especially my father had written down their childhood memories of life in the Island some 80 years ago. My father had a very hard life being poor and one of eight children and was brought up by his widowed mother. The stories he used to tell, the different aspects of life, and although he had a good and very hard working mother he received many hidings and bashings. He was quite a handful I believe, but it would have made very interesting reading! Being no angel and receiving so many bashings really did him no harm as he was a wonderful character — he thought a great deal of gran and he was a very good son to her right to the end of her days.

In 1940 everyone on the Island over the age of 14 had to fill in a Registration Form with all details of family records etc. Dated 28th October 1940 these records were for the issuing of 'Identity' cards which everyone had to always carry around or be fined by the Germans if they didn't. One question was asked 'Have you served in any of His Majesty's Armed Forces? If so, write RN, RNR, Army, RAF, Royal Guernsey Militia or as is appropriate and give your rank on retirement and the date of retirement. My father proudly filled in with 'Army Gunner' — Retirement 11/3/1920! He was only 16 years of age and was probably thrown out at the time! I remember him telling the story of being under the age (15) and lying about his age to get in the army. I shouldn't have thought he'd have had much time to train or to gun down anyone! (Luckily the Germans did ignore that statement!) He must have fooled the authorities at the time by his height, as he was well over 6ft., his brothers almost as tall. They were all Guernsey-born although not of Guernsey origin. Their father Edward Finigan was London born and was a seaman. He tragically fell between the ship and the quay in Alderney and was killed.

It is a well known fact that Guernsey people are short in stature. They have long bodies and short legs and are affectionately called Guernsey Donkeys (hence the picture page). They are also known to be stubborn. Jersey people are known as 'Crapauds' pronounced Crapows meaning toads or frogs. Thinking about the characters of the 'Collins' family I would say they were definitely the true Donkeys – not the 'Finigans', not in stature anyway!

Mother's stories would also have been of hard times as again, they the Collins were of a large family, and when Mum and Dad first married, I remember Mum saying how grateful she was to earn five shillings scrubbing shop floors. She worked hard with Dad too. Mum had three brothers and two sisters and I can only imagine a much quieter childhood with both parents. No holidays for mum, dad or any of the families, not even to Herm or Sark, even if there were day trips. I can remember mum talking of the 'Show Days' and the 'Races' (at L'Ancresse, I should think) — great days out for all the family and the 'Charabanc' rides. Similar for us would be after the War a drive or a picnic perhaps at Pleinmont? A crowd of us sitting in the back of dad's old 'bone shaker' — his working lorry, but we did have a lot of fun.

When mum was a small child, she had diphtheria and was very seriously ill in hospital. She finally had to have an operation 'a tracheotomy' — an opening of the windpipe to enable her to breathe. The scar was very noticeable throughout her life. All those years ago it must have been a very major operation and a great concern to gran and grandpa and she was very ill for a long time. After Liberation Day she completely lost her voice for many days and for weeks she could only whisper due to all the excitement, singing and emotion of the day. It was not due to smoking (she never did) but probably the weakness there from the operation. She always said it was the happiest day of her life and worth the silence! Do you know I can honestly say I have never seen my mother shout in anger or even get a little bad tempered in all her life, nor a grumble. Sad and worried, yes. Neither did I see her or her father — gramp, grandpa, Joe or Pop! Determination in what they wanted to do but never an argument or quarrel — nor with dad. They were so well suited and happy together.

Dad was advised by his doctor to retire when he was 60 years of age. He was in bed suffering with flu and because of this, a heart complaint had shown up. After sorting out his small business (but keeping on his employees for a while as he had a right-hand man he could rely on), he slowed up an awful lot. He gave up driving too and walked down to the harbour only occasionally. It was such a worry for mum as he had been such an active man but now he seemed to lose all confidence in himself. He carried with him his pills for angina but I'm sure he worried about himself when out and never ventured far.

It was in 1972 several years later that he suffered a heart attack and after three days being very ill and mum watching over him day and night with aunty Edie (Wilcox) he passed away. I don't remember mum being able to have a good cry — she used to comfort us but didn't want to see us cry either. 'Dad wouldn't want to see us cry' she'd say and she'd outwardly seem very strong. This I'm sure was most unfortunate as from then on she never seemed able to cry. She kept up so well — too well as she missed him so much. It was very fortunate we were living almost opposite as she stayed and slept with us whenever she wanted — mostly during winter-time when she felt his loss far more.

It was maybe two or three years later when Mother had a particular worry. It probably wouldn't have worried anyone else, but my uncle asked if she would attend a Court hearing and be a witness as he wanted a divorce. My aunt concerned realised their marriage was over and had accepted this, but my mother was so unhappy and sensitive towards aunty Rita whom she was very fond of that she just made herself sick over it. We had no idea this was troubling mum but we found her beginning to act in a very strange way and my sister and I were becoming more concerned over her. Time, days and clocks were on her mind all the time, she was counting constantly, very worried.

I was thinking and remembering aunty Al at this time (her sister), but our family doctor convinced us she would get better by keeping her at home amongst the caring family she had.

It was two or three days before the 'divorce' date that it suddenly dawned on Joyce and I what was troubling mum and we seemed to eventually get through to her, really, only on the very day. Then she started to improve and came 'back to us'. The nightmare fortnight seemed to be over and gradually she was her lovely old self again. A year or two later she took a holiday with aunty Edie to Yorkshire where originally she came from before living in Guernsey. We received letters from mum and she seemed to enjoy her holiday and meeting again all Edie's family. We were to meet them at the harbour but again mum was 'high and excitable' — and again this proved to be a worrying period. Mum came home to sleep so we could keep an eye on her, keeping company and just watching, as the doctor at that time couldn't seem to help her either with medicines or injections. She just wasn't our mum for two or three weeks again, but improvement eventually came.

After a fairly long while the family could not understand why mum seemed to be changing personality again, couldn't relax or sleep at all, very excitable and strong, doing strange things. Our very caring and patient family doctor then (Jones, who unfortunately for many now lives in England), decided she must have tests and a hospital stay. The blood tests showed mum was suffering from manic depression due to a shortage of 'lithium' in her body. This is a chemical (salt) which the doctors could treat then and nowadays by careful monitoring and frequently having blood tests. The medication would have to be carefully adjusted from time to time, being most important to keep her well. These stabilised her condition and fortunately although she had her 'high' and 'low' periods, she kept fairly well in between and for long periods, thanks due to many visits to our 'kindly' doctors.

Although Joyce and I knew mum would be well cared for at the Castel Hospital, it was always a sad ride in the car when both having to take her again, with always the worry of what the outcome could be. It really is a Hospital where the patients are very well looked after and loved, and we know mum was loved too. The nurses and staff do a wonderful job and together with many islanders who have had loved ones stay there, our sincere hope is, it will always be there to welcome the sick and mentally ill.

Her visiting Community Psychiatric nurse who came regularly often said to me 'that mum was really a remarkable lady' in the way she came back to pick up the threads after the 'manic' periods in hospital and in the way she continued with her life amongst us once again. I was of the opinion mostly it was worry and upset that would cause another bout so tried always to avoid any, where mum was concerned.

It was fairly obvious that after dad died mum would eventually live with us, especially now with her sickness. During dad's last three days he never spoke but he knew that he was seriously ill and that should anything happen to him, he would know and he would want us to be the ones to look after mum. She eventually came permanently in 1978 as she really needed company and loved having everyone around her. Sally, our elder daughter had moved over to her home at Rose Villa and mum was happy to move into Sally's bedroom. A good arrangement as mum could still pop over and know there was still the ever-open door to her. Apart from the first 10 years of married life, her home and heart had always been in 'Les Canichers' — at Rose Villa then at 'Woodcote' (formerly 'Rose Adele' from many years before). Altogether mum lived with us for almost 13 years.

CHAPTER 20

WITH 'CLIFF' A COINCIDENCE AT 'COOLDERRY'

Dad passed away at No. 30 in May 1972 (aged 68). My only regret now is that mum did not also end her days at home, but it was not to be. Unfortunate and sad but in some ways she spent a very contented last year of her life. It was early in 1990, although for only a minor operation, I had to go into the Princess Elizabeth Hospital — I daren't tell mum as black clouds would be over and she'd be most worried and upset if she had known. So the 'visiting' nurse and myself suggested she have a short stay at a nearby Residential Home. She agreed to have a look at it and as always agreed to go, as she felt André and I needed a break together. We had also mentioned we would be taking a holiday, and again this was usual for us, and although she was always a little sad saying 'goodbye', she wouldn't make us feel guilty about going. Little did we expect a big coincidence and a good deal of pleasure would come out of her stay at Coolderry House Residential Home!

From the very beginning it was noticeable that a resident 'Clifford Falla' took a liking to her and wanted to help her all he could. He loved chatting to her and she would make him laugh. When André and I returned after a couple of weeks we fully expected for ma to ask to come home, but she didn't, she just said she'd stay another week which the matron was quite happy about. Another week went by, then another and still she said the same and seemed happy enough.

The only grouse from ma was 'the others don't sing or dance at all' — she felt the grannies which she called them were too quiet! There were times when she tried livening them up and on taking her back after spending some time with us, would enter the lounge singing 'Here I am again — happy as can be ' — somehow contented again to be amongst the 'grannies' and Cliff. André's niece Yvonne was in charge of the Home so I'm sure she felt content that someone in the family was at hand. She settled in well and liked the company around her all day. Cliff always sat next to her and many times touched her hands lovingly, and you could see the way they looked at each other and laughed together they were enjoying each other's company.

Many a time when we called and mum was feeling up to it, they'd be sitting together in the garden holding hands. During the early morning when mum heard Cliff make his way downstairs, up she'd get and follow him into the lounge.

They'd greet each other with a kiss and a cuddle and then have a cup of tea waiting for the others to join them for breakfast. mum had never wanted nor looked for a male friend since dad had died in 1972 and this year was 1990. Neither had Cliff wanted female company and he had also been a widower for many years. I would describe him as a typical Guernsey- man, being short in stature but with a very big heart as he really was a kind man. He had worked in greenhouses growing tomatoes for most of his life except during the war years when he was in the Forces and for a time afterwards before returning to the Island. His job again took him into greenhouses working for many years with my uncle, Sid Collins, which we found out eventually through my aunt. Because of his kindness to mum (and all at the Home), she thought a lot of him and he in turn saw a little of mum's character of old. It was very sad and unfortunate that mum's health and physical condition deteriorated during the last few months and she couldn't always enjoy or feel like the outings they could have shared together. But the last time they were taken out together by Cliff's niece Joan was a happy time. Mum was heartily singing all her old cheery tunes during the afternoon with Cliff's family; he spoke of it so often. She was taken ill the next day and after two days in bed was taken to the Princess Elizabeth Hospital very poorly and dehydrated. Mum had been at the Home then for eleven months and during all this time she still did not ask to come home.

When she showed a slight improvement I wondered whether Cliff would like to visit mum. He was delighted of course and I used to collect him around 3.30 p.m. and we'd both go together to the Princess Elizabeth Hospital every day, Joyce would visit earlier.

He would stay on until the nurses prepared mum for bed around 6.00 p.m. or just after. It was touching though as he never wanted to leave, he was so content to sit and look at her the whole time. 'Florence' a very kind and helpful lady who was in the next bed to Mum was often tearful (me also of course) as she couldn't help but hear the loving and tender words between them. Sometimes at 'Coolderry' mum would think Cliff silly to show he cared and would tell us; but she always spoke of him as her 'number one' and vice versa. I shall never again believe that love is only for the young, it was a very touching experience for me to see.

The very strange coincidence occurred at this time. It was a day I collected Cliff from his sister-in-law whom he had joined for Sunday lunch. As I walked in, she called my name and said she hadn't seen me for many years. Although I had seen this lady around the town, I never knew her name, nor knew her. As I was leaving with Cliff, I noticed a wedding picture on the wall and remarked of it as I recognised Cliff as the groom. Strange too, I seemed to have remembered his wife in the photograph and mentioned this to Cliff. The sister-in-law then asked if I knew who the young girl was, the bridesmaid in the picture. I was amazed, it was me!! Yes, the familiar dress and headdress and the floral material (which I still had) of course it was me — but what a surprise and a big coincidence. In my old photograph album was a photo of me on my own as a bridesmaid in 1939 — but no bride and groom. I often wondered who they could have been and only knew they were relations of mum and dad's friends. Nothing more. To be Cliff of all people! Now I could understand, as when mum and dad married, their first home was a tiny three roomed cottage in St. John's Street with two other small cottages situated around a small courtyard/garden. In one of the cottages Cliff's sister, husband and daughter Pam lived. Seeing Pam (his niece) and I were around the same age and always playing together it was possible there was no-one else so I was asked to join her as well. I must have been excited to oblige as I was aged seven or eight and a bridesmaid for the first time. I'm so pleased I know the full story now and to have the group wedding photograph which Cliff gave to me soon afterwards.

Thinking back I realised mum had said several times 'you're the bridesmaid, eh Molly?' but I used to just laugh and say 'oh yes Mum I'll be your bridesmaid on the big day'. Never realizing what she meant, but Cliff (through his sister-in-law) had realised who I was and had told mum, but I just had taken it the wrong way. Strange how coincidences occur after many years, over 50 in fact, and to think it had to be Cliff to help her and give her the special company she needed in those last few months. For the first time since dad had died she wasn't just relying on me and the family. André has always felt Cliff did more good for her than all the medicines (with many varieties she had to take) put together.

Mum was very tired and frail on leaving the hospital but seemed to be content to return to Coolderry House. Her eyesight was failing and despite having a cataract operation the previous year, other problems due to her age had developed and the condition was worsening. She never grumbled but she was certainly weaker now and within two days of coming home she was confined to bed. During the next month or so I should have known the end was near, but I never did. I just felt mum had been with us for so long and I suppose at 86 years she would go on

147

forever. There might have been something she said in the hospital I should have heeded — she had mentioned wanting to go on a long journey by train ('just you and me' she said) to Canada. Then a couple of times she said she was walking in 'God's beautiful garden'. Although not particularly religious I can hear her now saying her prayers out loud as she did every night. Another time she spoke of going home to her mum and dad, all signs I suppose I should have known. After being restless for a day or two, it was the kind Matron of the Home who jolted me when she said she felt mum would probably last until maybe 1.00 or 2.00 a.m. Mum did slip quietly away at that time and my sister and I were with her. I'm grateful that we do have the consolation of knowing mother never asked to come home and always seemed content to be amongst the caring staff. Even when she came home to us for a meal or just a car ride she was always ready and happy to go back. The Matron and her husband, Mr. and Mrs. Crispini, Yvonne and all the staff cared for mum and showed many kindnesses right to the end, she couldn't have been better looked after. One good lady, a night duty 'nurse' also called Phyl has spoken to me only recently and told me the reason she resigned and left her job at the Home was because mum wasn't there any more. She missed her so much. Apparently they used to have a little sing-song together and got on well together; like the rest of the staff they all loved 'Gladys' which everyone knew her as.

André and I expected a good number of family friends to attend mother's funeral at St. John's Church, the parish church where all mum's family had been christened and buried, but on entering the

Pleinmont
12 Feb 1991.

My Dear Molly & Joyce,
My thoughts are with you
today — and my love too.
How lucky you both are
to have such lovely memories
of such a gorgeous Mum (and
Dad) I am sure now they
are together once more — and
if they have such things in
Heaven — she will be "robbing
his money bags" in the wardrobe
remember?
She gave so much of
herself to others always, to
will always be remembered
for her goodness and above
all her sense of fun.

Love you both old friends
Peg

Church a minute or two before the service began it is difficult for me to explain how I felt. The Church seemed to be packed, so many wanting to pay tribute to mum. Inside me, a big surge or pride and sadness at the same time. I really wanted there and then to hug and thank everyone for attending. Even the wreaths and floral tributes wanted to keep blooming for her, they were several weeks old before they faded and died. André and I received over a hundred touching and sympathetic letters and cards which I shall always treasure. Others with a touch of humour which just had to be, remembering mum (and dad).

Peggy (née Bodkin) the Vazon Bay and 'Telephone Exchange' friend used to be one of many who visited our home those many years ago and she remembered the laughs shared with mum raiding dad's pockets, his money bags and the good times of old with us all.

Never thinking mum was so ill, Cliff was shocked and badly shaken knowing mum had passed away. Whenever I visited him after, he would talk of Mrs. Finigan, the lovely lady he still missed. Being very helpful and chatty at the Home, and always dressed cleanly and very smart other ladies were always interested in him but no — he used to say to Yvonne 'its only Mrs. Finigan I might have married', and who knows what might have happened if they had met two or three years earlier. Now sadly our Cliff has passed away too and for me to visit 'Coolderry' brings back the sad but also very warm and contented memories of them both together.

CHAPTER 21

CONCLUSIONS

I have been most fortunate during my lifetime and in many ways. First and foremost having wonderful parents, caring daughters, family and many good friends. So fortunate too in having a loving husband André, and for him understanding mum's illness and his support at all times. There were many happy years and times whilst mum lived with us but at times I could not have coped without his help and patience. Especially so as he like many others had to come to terms with certain disabilities for over 20 years and hasn't always felt well himself.

Our four grandchildren, Ryan, Carly, Joshua and Naomi are the bestest, anywhere!

Grateful I was born in this Island of Guernsey and in this road we are still living. If I hadn't I would not have enjoyed nor would I have been able to appreciate the view from our back windows each morning. At sunrise the sun peeps and rises over the Island of Herm and Sark or at different times, between. With the changing colour of the sky some mornings and during the light evenings, I have often wished I was an artist and could paint the scene as the Islands change colour too, sometimes an orangy glow, sometimes Herm will look mauve and purple. I often wonder what dad would have thought of the view if he could come back. He always admired and loved the view too but unfortunately the massive car park is there and I'm sure he wouldn't be impressed at the first sight. But saying that, looking beyond the harbour and Castle Cornet the Islands and the sea can still be seen, also Alderney and Jersey. On clear days and evenings we can even see the coast and attractive lights on France (Flamanville) and sometimes the buildings on the coast. The one view that all islanders miss is the one when driving down St. Julian's Avenue, one is faced with a roundabout and cars — more cars in place of the blue sea and islands. It really was a beautiful sight especially so with our very high tides, but sadly gone for always now.

André has always appreciated the view from home too like he says

View from Les Cotils, the QEII marina being built 1984/85. Woodcote left hand corner.

— with so many boats coming and going it is an ever changing picture and it is never taken for granted by either of us. He feels now that we are older, we should move to a smaller house. With so many rooms there is always work to be done and the upkeep is expensive seeing he cannot hope to do it all (just recently reached the Senior Citizen age!) During 1974 we had built quite a large extension at the back of the house and we've recently had permission for a self catering holiday unit — I shall now keep my fingers crossed for it to be a success as like the 'Collin's' (mum and gramp) before me, I don't want to move, not yet anyway. Where else is there a 'Canichers' and a 'view'? I would be very fussy if I had to choose.

My memories are now stored and now by writing to and for you and getting it down on paper it will have helped me to get the recent sad past out of my system, not my thoughts, could never do that. You will now know a little more about my family and friends too, and of Guernsey over the years. I hope you will forgive me for perhaps not having all this in perfect order and perhaps a repeat here and there. I also hope you will have found the reading of our family characters of interest despite having perhaps had no recollection of my memoirs written in a 'A Child's War' previously. With my 'Reflections' over 50 years it has not been so easy to remember and write about. With 'A Child's War' looking back it really was a small but very important and

At a friends wedding 1992.

memorable time in all our lives. I remember 'Erich' my German friend writing and saying it was the greatest tribute I could have done to write about my mother like I have, now I feel my dear father is included in my tribute and I'm sure he would have been very pleased with my effort. I truly never ever expected my book to be such a success and when mum and I chatted I used to say 'thousands of people have read about you ma'— she would always smile and with a little laugh poo-pooed it, but I know the car rides we had together always gave great pleasure. With me distributing copies she would always be asking during the season. 'Any more books wanted at the shops?' I don't think she ever realised what a great character she was, especially so when younger having to look after six hungry working men, herself, myself and sister; always so cheerfully running the home, worrying constantly about each day's meals and where to get something, and then caring for everyone around her. It didn't help either as she really was frightened of the invading enemy and they were everywhere, just couldn't get away from them at all.

Two years have gone by since mum died — 10th February 1991 — aged 86 years (a coincidence that her dad 'Gramp' had also died the same day and month). As I am writing the final page — it's 10.30 a.m. and the door bell has just rung and I have been handed a box of beautiful carnations. Sent by a dear friend and visitor from years ago

Ken Bernhardt of Beckenham, Kent being one of the 'Three Puds' of whom the other two, Freda and Jim Banks, also of Beckenham, had sent a bouquet last year also on the 10th February. Remembering us, and especially mum on this day. Time has passed quickly but even to mum thinking back over 50 years when her mum (my gran) passed away, it seemed to her only like yesterday. Whenever she spoke of her, it was always with a tear in her eye. Over the years she had always spoken of her, and I know I shall always miss mum too. I'm sure the feeling amongst us all are the same for loved ones who have left us. So many times there is a reminder. Life is precious and it is tragic to see lives taken for no good reason whatsoever in different parts of the world over recent months, even years. Mum, André and I had a lovely holiday together after dad died in the 70s and have seen parts of Yugoslavia, and what a wonderful country it was. I can hardly believe what's happening now with horrific tales and terrible sadness and suffering amongst so many of its people. Terribly sad for everyone, young and old. It would be lovely to think should there be further 'Reflections' of life to write about, it could be of everyone having peace and contentment with each other like the majority of us over recent years have enjoyed. Should I ever write another long letter (as this has been to me) in a few years' time, I sincerely hope it will again be memories of the happy times and of nice people — my kind of people.

A La Prochaine

On finishing the last few words must be of dear mum — who everybody knew and loved as you will have probably gathered. I recently came across a letter written to her in the early 30's by W. M. Martin, then manager of Gardner's Royal Hotel on the Esplanade.

"THE CRABPOT"
Guernsey, Channel Islands.

Dear little Miss Funny Face,
The enclosed is a simple token from me in appreciaton of your "Funny Face", and may anything you produce be as good as you.
All Happiness to you and yours,
From Old WM (W. Martin)

Mr Martin employed mum and she temporarily had to give up her waitress work for a bundle. I do hope it was me who eventually arrived and that I can boast perhaps even to a quarter of mum's special qualities, and to a little of her always cheerful "funny face"!